USC FOOTBALL
YESTERDAY & TODAY™

DAVID WHARTON
FOREWORD BY JOHN ROBINSON

WEST
SIDE
PUBLISHING

David Wharton has covered sports for the *Los Angeles Times* for 25 years. His work has won a range of national honors, including the Associated Press Sports Editors Award, and has been selected for the Best American Sports Writing series. He has also written for magazines such as *Surfer* and *Men's Fitness* and has coauthored another book on USC football titled *Conquest*.

John Robinson coached the USC Trojans for two stints that spanned from 1976 to 1997, guiding the team to eight bowl games and a national championship. He also coached at UNLV and in the NFL, where he led the Los Angeles Rams to the playoffs in six of his nine seasons. Since retiring from the game, he has worked as a broadcaster and is a member of the Master Coaches Survey.

Factual verification by Patrick Garbin

Special thanks to the Newport Sports Museum, a nonprofit 501(c)(3) sports memorabilia and educational center dedicated to mentoring at-risk youth and preserving the history of sport. In 1993, John W. Hamilton established the museum by putting his vast collection on display, free of charge to the public. Now considered one of the world's largest, the collection is used merely as a vehicle to motivate children to stay in school, become involved in athletics, and stay away from drugs and gangs.

We would also like to thank Claude Zachary from the USC Archives.

"Fight On" lyrics reprinted with permission by Sweet Music.

Front cover: Reggie Bush carries the ball against Washington State in 2004. **Back cover:** The USC football team rushes out of the tunnel before the 2007 Rose Bowl.

Yesterday & Today is a trademark of Publications International, Ltd.

West Side Publishing is a division of Publications International, Ltd.

ISBN-13: 978-1-4127-6090-4
ISBN-10: 1-4127-6090-9

Manufactured in China.

8 7 6 5 4 3 2 1

Library of Congress Control Number: 2009923892

Picture credits:

Front cover: ***Sports Illustrated*/Getty Images**

Back cover: © John Pyle/Icon SMI/Corbis

Alamy Images: ArtPix, 33 (bottom); **AP Images:** 7 (left), 23, 28 (right), 29 (bottom), 35, 40 (right & bottom), 44 (left), 46, 49 (bottom), 50, 53, 57 (bottom), 59 (bottom), 61 (top), 69 (left), 81 (bottom), 89 (right), 108, 111, 113 (left), 115, 116, 123, 125, 128 (left), 132, 134 (left); © **Corbis:** contents, Bettmann, 6, 25, 27 (left), 40 (top), 68 (right), 81 (top); Mike Blake/Reuters, 127 (bottom); Darryl Dennis/Icon SMI, 127 (top); Robert Galbraith/Reuters, 113 (right); Ben Liebenberg, endsheets, 106, 128 (right); Lucy Nicholson/Reuters, 118 (left); Rick Scuteri/Reuters, 112; Marc Serota/Reuters, 100; Tim Tadder, 103; Chris Williams/Icon SMI, 130, 135 (right); **Getty Images:** 80, 83, 88, 89 (left), 90 (top center), 92, 93, 94, 95 (left), 96 (left), 110, 114, 117, 119, 126, 129, 131, 133, 135 (left); Collegiate Images, contents, 27 (right), 58 (right), 66 (left), 76 (bottom), 87 (top); *Sports Illustrated*, 3, 49 (top), 56, 58 (left), 64 (top left), 67 (right), 68 (left), 69 (right), 72, 74 (left), 75, 77 (right), 79, 95 (right), 97, 101, 102, 122, 124; Time Life Pictures, 67 (left), 99 (left center); **Los Angeles Public Library:** 24 (left); Paul Chinn/*Herald-Examiner* Collection, 78 (left); Chris Gulker/*Herald-Examiner* Collection, 70 (right); Tom LaBonge/*Herald-Examiner* Collection, 71; Serigo Ortiz/*Herald-Examiner* Collection, 61 (bottom); James Roark/*Herald-Examiner* Collection, 73 (top); James Ruebsamen/*Herald-Examiner* Collection, 82; **Newport Sports Museum:** contents, 7 (right), 8 (left), 18 (top left & bottom), 19, 24 (right), 29 (top), 30, 31 (top left, top center, top right & bottom right), 37 (bottom), 38 (top left & bottom), 39 (bottom left & bottom right), 44 (right), 47 (left), 48 (top), 54 (bottom right), 55 (top right), 57 (top), 63 (bottom), 64 (top right), 65 (top left & bottom), 74 (right), 78 (right), 84 (left), 85 (bottom left), 86 (right), 90 (top right), 91 (top left & bottom right), 96 (right), 98 (top right), 99 (top left), 104 (top right), 121 (top left & bottom right), 136 (left & bottom), 137 (left center), 140; **NFL:** 48 (bottom), 66 (right); **PIL Collection:** 22 (left), 31 (bottom left), 38 (top right), 39 (top left & top right), 54 (top left, top right & bottom left), 55 (top left, bottom left & bottom right), 59 (top), 64 (bottom left & bottom right), 65 (right), 70 (left), 77 (left), 84 (top right & bottom right), 85 (top left, top right & bottom right), 87 (bottom), 90 (top left & bottom), 91 (top right & bottom left), 98 (top left & bottom), 99 (top right & bottom), 104 (top left, bottom left & bottom right), 105 (top left & bottom left), 109 (bottom), 120 (left & center), 121 (bottom left & top right), 137 (top left, right & bottom left), 139; **Hans Tesselaar:** 105 (right), 118 (right), 120 (right), 134 (right), 136 (center); **Courtesy University of Southern California, on behalf of the USC Archives:** 8 (right), 9, 10, 11, 12, 13, 14, 15, 16, 17, 18 (top right), 20, 21, 22 (right), 26, 28 (left), 32, 33 (top), 34, 36, 37 (top), 41, 42, 43, 47 (right), 51, 60, 63 (top), 73 (bottom), 109 (top); USC Athletic Department, 62; **WireImage:** contents, 45, 52, 76 (top), 86 (left), 107

Additional photography: Timothy O'Leary; PDR Productions, Inc./Peter Rossi

USC's cheerleaders, in their crisp white sweaters, pose before the beginning of the 2008 Rose Bowl. USC beat Penn State 38–24. The day belonged to Mark Sanchez, who became only the third quarterback to pass for more than 400 yards in a Rose Bowl game.

Contents

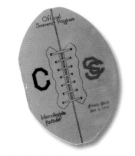

1919 football program, page 8

John Wayne, page 27

John McKay, page 52

Ronnie Lott, page 87

Game day, page 130

USC Trojans: Yesterday and Today

Foreword by John Robinson

John Robinson was inducted into the College Football Hall of Fame in 2009.

Each of us treasure those special moments that make up our own history with USC football. I've had my share. My personal history with the Trojans came when I was a sophomore in college. The University of Oregon had come to play 'SC at the Coliseum. I was awed by the size of everything. The venue was huge. There were 80,000 people in the stands. The Spirit of Troy marching band looked like an army. Their mascot, Traveler, was a super-size horse. Then there were the linemen . . . . We lost.

Some years later I returned to the Coliseum, not as a player but as the defensive coordinator for U. of Oregon. My job was to stop the running game of the defending national champion Trojans and a back named O. J. Simpson . . . . We lost.

In 1972, I got to come back to USC not as an opponent but as part of the coaching staff. I was hired by head coach John McKay. John became my boss, my mentor, and my friend all in the same year. It was an amazing experience and has made me a Trojan for life. That team went 12–0, took the national championship, and was perhaps the best ever. We had a gifted fullback in Sam "Bam" Cunningham. He was our goal-line runner, and he had a characteristic move that we called "Sam Over the Top." I never got tired of watching Sam take the football, dive over the defense, and score. In the 1973 Rose Bowl, we enjoyed a decisive victory over Ohio State with "Sam Over the Top" for four touchdowns.

Two years later we were back in the Rose Bowl, again for the national championship, and again facing Ohio State. Our quarterback was Pat Haden, and Johnny McKay Jr. was his favorite receiver. Those young men had played together in high school and continued the tradition of "Haden to McKay" into college. Pat, Johnny, and I worked hard that year on a special play we called "Play Pass-X Corner." We used to bug coach McKay to call that play in practice, we were just sure it would work, but he would just grumble. Late in the Rose Bowl game, USC was behind. It was first and ten at midfield. Coach McKay called a timeout to talk to his son Johnny, Pat, and me. "Okay boys, let's run it," was all he had to say. We did. We scored . . . . We won.

I took over as head coach in 1976 and participated in some of my own unforgettable moments. One of my "best" plays came that year against UCLA. Vince Evans, our QB, had struggled his junior year, but this was his moment. It was all on the line: the game, the Victory Bell, a trip to the

Players hoist Robinson on their shoulders after defeating Ohio State 17–16 in the 1980 Rose Bowl.

Rose Bowl. The play we used was our "Quarterback Draw." Vince, running that play, is seared forever in my brain. Vince took off, blasting his way right through the Bruin defense for 34 yards and a touchdown . . . . We won.

The year 1978 is one I'll never forget. That year we were co-national champions. We shared the title with the University of Alabama, a team we had defeated earlier in the season 24–12. The 1978 Rose Bowl pitted USC against Ohio State. We were behind late in the game and 82 yards away from a touchdown. It looked like a very long way to go so I decided to go with our best and most consistent players. I had the QB give the ball to Charles White and had Anthony Munoz, our All-America tackle, blocking for him. We continued to run that play right down the field to a fourth and one on the Buckeye 1-yard line. What play to call? How about White behind Munoz. It worked. White scored . . . . We won.

Another great memory is from the 1981 season. Our quarterback, John Mazur, and I shared that moment in the game against Oklahoma. It was an early season game, between two top-ranked teams. Both John and I knew how important this game was. It was a hard-fought game that came right down to the wire. We trailed by six points with three seconds left. There were 100,000 people watching in the stadium and hundreds of thousands more watching on national television as John and I huddled on the sideline. It was a tense moment. Mazur was scared to death, as was I. I wanted John to relax so he could do what he had to do. I decided to tell him a joke, a really stupid joke. We both laughed even though he thought I was crazy. On that last play, Mazur went out and threw a pass for a touchdown....We won.

There are hundreds of great moments in USC football history. Some are in the collective memory: like the last-second victory over Notre Dame with "Fertig to Sherman." Or more recently, "Leinart's Quarterback Sneak." I'm sure you have your own personal favorites. Enjoy reliving those moments in this great book.

Fight On!

John Robinson

John Robinson

Robinson compiled an impressive 104–35–4 record in two stints coaching for USC. He signed this football for a lucky fan.

Our Alma Mater Dear

1888–1924

Long before the I formation and "Student Body Right," before the Rose Bowl, seven Heisman trophies, and eleven national championships, a group of USC students gathers on campus to try their hand at an odd-looking sport. The grand tradition of Trojan football is born.

Near left: *The 1907 football team, like others of its era, played a patchwork schedule against squads from local colleges, high schools, and military bases. Harvey Holmes served as the university's first paid coach and helped to establish a rivalry with Stanford to the north.* **Far left:** *This program is from the 1916 California–USC game.*

The Trojans finish their 1921 season with a 10–1 record, defeating Washington State 28–7 before a crowd of 18,000 at Tournament Park in Pasadena. Charley Dean is the team's right halfback and captain.

A Strange New Game

Through the early years, college football was a game of ever-changing rules, played by ragtag teams. In 1909, USC fights to a 0–0 tie against nearby Pomona.

Los Angeles remained something of a frontier town in the 1880s, with modern conveniences such as paved streets and electricity still an oddity. But the city had a major academic institution, the University of Southern California, and by 1888 that school had a football team. A student named Arthur Carroll not only organized the first team of players, but as a future tailor he also sewed their pants.

In those days, American football blended elements of rugby and soccer on a field 110 yards long, not including the end zones. Touchdowns counted as four points, the

official time was subject to debate, and players were considered too rough if they tackled below the waist. There were no leagues or conferences in the area, so the fledgling USC team had only one opponent: the Alliance Athletic Club of Los Angeles.

The teams first met on campus in mid-November, with USC prevailing 16–0. Two months later, in January 1889, they held a rematch on a vacant lot bordered by Grand Avenue and Hope Street. "The club team had improved considerably and we managed to score only a single touchdown to win 4–0," said Harry Lillie—an end who weighed all of 125 pounds—in the book *The Trojan Heritage*. With that, USC had recorded its first undefeated season.

As years passed, football persevered in fits and starts led by a variety of player-coaches or, occasionally, no coach at all. The team skipped a couple seasons, in part because the university set down stricter rules, concerned that some young men were enrolling simply to play the game and not for want of knowledge. It was the students who kept football alive.

The Methodists—or the Wesleyans, as they called themselves—arranged games against reputable squads from Pomona and Occidental while also padding their record with victories over Whittier Reform School, the California National Guard's 7th Regiment, and the Phoenix Indian School. When Loyola forfeited after an argument about the time allotted for each half in 1904, USC settled for competing against prep students. A year later, when the local Harvard School arrived short-handed, the home team loaned its coach to the other side.

Eight years after USC was founded, Henry Goddard and Frank Suffel coached the university's first football team. The makeshift squad played only two games in 1888, winning both, against a local athletic club.

USC football gained a stronger foothold in the late 1890s when Lewis Freeman took over as the first non-playing coach, dressing his athletes in knee-length pants and turtlenecks, with the school's letters stitched neatly across their chests. The first salaried coach, Harvey Holmes, arrived in 1904 as the schedule gradually expanded from a couple of games to as many as ten a year. USC almost always finished with a winning record, led by early stars such as Harold Paulin, Court Decius, and Elwin Caley who, playing on that extra-long field, still holds the school record for returning a kick 107 yards, which happened against Pomona in 1902.

Year by year, the team went looking for stronger competition. Holmes took his players north for an inaugural game against highly regarded Stanford in 1905. Not long after, coach Dean Cromwell guided USC to a 7–0–1 record in 1910, its most successful season to date. Future

"Splendid Fighting Spirit"

As college nicknames go, the USC Methodists wasn't exactly catchy. Neither was the other name—the Wesleyans—that USC's teams answered to in the early days. It took a suggestion by *Los Angeles Times* sportswriter Owen Bird to provide a moniker that stuck.

Summoned to the university in 1912, Bird recalled telling an administrator that "the athletes and coaches of the university were under terrific handicaps. They were facing teams that were bigger and better equipped, yet they had splendid fighting spirit. The name 'Trojans' fitted [sic] them."

The nickname passed its first test in a newspaper article published before USC played Stanford, and it soon began to spread. Bird said: "The term 'Trojan' as applied to USC means to me that no matter what the situation, what the odds or what the conditions, the competition must be carried on to the end and those who strive must give all they have and never be weary in doing so."

conference opponents such as Oregon State (in 1914), California (1915), and Arizona (1916) were added to the schedule.

Football had not only survived at USC, it had prospered with crowds as large as 10,000 gathering to watch the games. But the team would face one more test—and nearly be disbanded forever—before establishing itself as a national powerhouse in the college game's golden era.

The Maker of Champions

Dean Cromwell held to a simple philosophy when it came to coaching football—he believed in hard work.

It might seem odd at a school known for football, but USC's first big-name coach was famous for a different sport. Dean Cromwell took the helm in 1909 and 1910, then he returned for three more seasons beginning in 1916. His 21–8–6 record included victories over Utah and Stanford and a tie against California, but those numbers paled in comparison to his success on the track.

The man known alternately as "The Dean" and the "Maker of Champions" had been a multisport athlete at Occidental College, and he spent a number of years working for the telephone company before coaching.

Through the first half of the 20th century, he led USC to a dozen NCAA track and field championships, including a remarkable stretch of nine consecutive titles from 1935 to 1943. His disciples included Charlie Paddock, Mel Patton, future USC track coach Vern Wolfe, and Frank Wykoff. At least one Cromwell athlete competed in every Summer Olympics from 1912 through 1948, winning 10 gold medals and setting 17 world records along the way. The school eventually named its track after him.

On the football field, Cromwell took a simple approach. "I will work them hard," he told the *Los Angeles Times* before his second stint with the Trojans in 1916, taking the reins of a team that had played poorly the season before. "Give them one thing at a time, but push them." It must have worked, because the Trojans rebounded for a 5–3 record that year, winning their finale against Arizona.

His last season started slowly, the schedule delayed when officials banned public gatherings in October 1918 because of an influenza outbreak. USC went 2–2–2 that year, and Cromwell also coached basketball. Thereafter, the future track Hall of Famer turned from football to his specialty. According to one newspaper account, he died in 1962 while watching a Green Bay Packers game.

A More Dignified Sport

Football wasn't always king at USC. In 1911, university administrators wanted a more dignified sport to complement their academic mission. According to the book *The Trojan Heritage,* they followed the lead of schools such as Stanford and California that had fielded teams in the venerable English game of rugby. A university spokesman explained: "We are looking for a foothold on an athletic ladder that will carry us, we hope, to a level of competition to the proportion of our ambitious, restless, growing young institution."

The USC rugby team in 1913, during a school-imposed hiatus for football.

From 1911 to 1913, football disappeared as the rugby team floundered. Those years weren't a complete loss—the squad's determination inspired a new nickname, the Trojans, and football came roaring back from its hiatus in 1914.

Gloomy Gus and Happy Times

The man who led the Trojans to national prominence was an unlikely figure by the name of Elmer C. Henderson. A successful high school coach in Seattle, Henderson took over at USC in 1919 and was immediately tagged "Gloomy Gus"—after a cartoon character—because he always downplayed his team's chances. "If Pomona doesn't beat us by six or seven touchdowns, I'll be a much surprised man," he told the *Los Angeles Times* before his first game. "I haven't a football player on the squad."

USC won that game 6–0, and it soon became apparent that, with Henderson, first impressions could be deceiving. Photographs from the era show a bespectacled figure with a clipped smile, dressed conservatively in a bowtie and sweater. In fact, Henderson was both genial and determined, characteristics that made him an aggressive recruiter. After bringing guard Leo Calland and other talented players from Seattle, he began stockpiling his roster with all the best high school prospects in Southern California. But talent was only half the story. Henderson also proved to be a savvy tactician, credited with inventing an early form of the spread offense that remains part of the game to this day.

College football was coming of age in the Roaring Twenties with the maturation of conferences and a scattering of postseason games. Henderson guided the Trojans to their first ten-win season in 1921 and, the next year, took them to the Rose Bowl, where for the first time they played a school east of the Rocky Mountains, defeating famed coach Hugo Bezdek and Penn State 14–3.

There were other firsts during Henderson's tenure. USC joined the Pacific Coast Conference and later moved to the newly constructed Los Angeles Memorial Coliseum in 1923, a shift that significantly boosted the team's annual revenue. In 1924, the Trojans enhanced their national reputation against two intersectional opponents, shutting out Syracuse in the regular-season finale before defeating Missouri in the Christmas Festival game.

That victory would be Henderson's last as a Trojan. Despite a 45–7 record over six years—not to mention stints coaching baseball and basketball—he was fired before the start of the 1925 season. Most reports blamed his five losses without a win against California. Regardless, Henderson still ranks as the most successful coach in USC history with an .865 winning percentage.

Elmer "Gloomy Gus" Henderson may have worn a dour look on his face, but he proved to be an enthusiastic recruiter and a savvy technician when it came to coaching football at USC.

> "If Pomona doesn't beat us by six or seven touchdowns, I'll be a much surprised man."
>
> "Gloomy Gus" Henderson

Going to the Game

By the early 1920s, USC games were drenched in all the color and pageantry we have come to expect from college football. Whereas the team once attracted several hundred curious onlookers, big rivalries now drew crowds as large as 20,000 to watch the likes of Charley Dean, Holly Adams, and Gordon Campbell play on Saturday afternoons. There was enough fan interest to justify scheduling doubleheaders, and some games had to be shifted to larger venues, such as Tournament Park in Pasadena.

Homecoming celebrations in 1921 were a particularly grand affair, encompassing a home game against Pomona followed by a trip north the following week to face rival California. Newspaper accounts tell of some fans caravaning by car while others rode on electric trains to the Wilmington docks, where they boarded a prewar ship called the *Yale* for the passage to Berkeley. There were game-day luncheons and a chapel rally that raised $500 to send along a 30-piece marching band.

It wasn't just football that prompted such enthusiasm. That band played on the field—"Fight On" and "All Hail" were composed during this era—as fans performed card stunts in the stands. Halfway through the 1922 season, with the Trojans making their way toward the Rose Bowl, an estimated 3,000 alumni gathered at Bovard Field the night before the Cal game. They paraded down University Avenue holding aloft a stuffed bear that was buried with great ceremony on campus. According to the *Los Angeles Times*, a bonfire and "a real barbecue followed this spectacle. Several large quarters of beef, a ton or so of beans and 3,000 French loaves were consumed, while the red and blue fire played its colors on the large crowd. Everybody predicted a victory for the University of Southern California by two touchdowns."

Local businesses got into the act, too. On the eve of the 1922 Thanksgiving Day game against Washington State, a local auto dealer supplied the team with a fleet of Maxwell motorcars so that players could be ferried to Pasadena's Hotel Maryland, where they spent the night in quarters far more luxurious than anything found at the dormitories. The Trojans had become a very public symbol for the university, building an impressive reputation for themselves. Now they needed a conference and a stadium to match.

An early version of the Trojan marching band performed at games in 1921.

A Vote of Approval

The year 1921 marked USC's 29th season of playing football. The Trojans were closing in on their 100th victory—they were a force to be reckoned with along the West Coast—and Elmer "Gloomy Gus" Henderson had established himself as a first-rate coach. It was time for the team to join a league of suitable standing.

The Pacific Coast Conference, established during a meeting at the Oregon Hotel in Portland six years earlier, needed a few more members to fill out its ranks. The PCC was overloaded with schools such as Washington, Washington State, Oregon, and Oregon State to the north. Travel constraints forced its southern constituents—California and Stanford—to settle for only a few league games each season. They wanted competition closer to home.

The Trojans were already playing one or two PCC teams a season, but concerns about whether they would adhere to the conference's strict academic standards had led to Stanford reportedly blocking their admission during closed-door sessions in 1920. Such concern about inappropriate behavior in college football would ultimately prove justified—a scandal later rocked several teams, including USC, UCLA, Cal, and Washington, leading to the dissolution of the conference in the late 1950s.

But in December 1921, these fears remained in the background as Stanford administrators relented, allowing Henderson to attend the PCC's annual gathering in Portland with full support of the membership. A subsequent vote passed unanimously. Officials welcomed USC and, to the surprise of many outsiders, the smaller, less-established Idaho as well. The meeting also produced an important

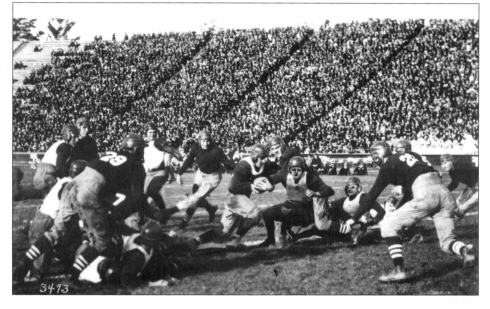

rule regarding the Rose Bowl, then still known as the "East-West" game. The conference did not like that a private entity, namely the Tournament of Roses committee, controlled the annual postseason event in Pasadena, and so they demanded authority to choose the contestants.

The Trojans made their PCC debut in late October 1922, losing 12–0 in a home game against Cal, a team that Henderson could never seem to handle. But after that less-than-sparkling debut, they ran the table with victories over Stanford, Idaho, and Washington State, finishing the regular season with a 9–1 record that included seven shutouts. When the first-place Golden Bears declined an invitation from the Tournament of Roses, the conference selected USC to face Penn State before a crowd of 43,000 on New Year's Day.

Playing their first season as a member of the Pacific Coast Conference in 1922, the Trojans eked out a 6–0 win over Stanford.

Trojans Find a Home

On a work site just south of the university, crews form giant dirt mounds into the shape of the Coliseum. The famed peristyle arches have already been erected.

Not long after halfback Charley Dean led the Trojans to a 28–7 victory over Washington State in the 1921 season finale, capping the first ten-win campaign in school history, an equally momentous occasion took place across the street from campus. On December 21, workers gathered at an abandoned gravel pit to break ground on the Los Angeles Memorial Coliseum.

So many years later, the Olympic torch that burns over the stadium's famous peristyle arches might lead fans to believe it was erected for the 1932 Summer Games. But Chris Epting, who researched the venue for his book, *Los Angeles Memorial Coliseum*, says that wasn't the case. "It was really an all-purpose center for L.A., a place where you could have religious ceremonies and soccer, everything," Epting said. "As time went on, of course, football became the prominent thing."

Working from plans drawn by architects John and Donald Parkinson, crews used dirt from the bottom of the pit to form the stadium's bowl shape, as if making a giant sand castle on the 17-acre site. They situated the peristyle's 15 arches—the center one stands 44 feet high, the others reaching to 26 feet—on the eastern end. Rows of bench sets were installed to accommodate 76,000 spectators, or roughly 13 percent of the city's population of approximately 576,000.

By today's standards, the $954,872 price tag seems ridiculously cheap. Even more surprising, construction finished in less than two years. "Fast and under budget," Epting said. "It's still a marvel of efficiency." In the decades that followed, the Coliseum would undergo extensive renovations, including the addition of 25,000 seats for the '32 Games and a facelift for the return of the Olympics in 1984. But by the fall of 1923, the stadium in its earliest version was ready to welcome USC football.

Let's Play Two

USC's first game at the Coliseum, October 6, 1923, fell somewhere short of a grand spectacle. Aerial photographs show the stadium in its simplest form, with a slanted earth facade around the outside instead of concrete. The field was pushed to the far western end of the bowl, where players emerged from the tunnel. "That was really early in the stadium's history," researcher and author Chris Epting said, "before it was redesigned for the 1932 Olympics."

The Trojans had yet to start drawing big crowds on a regular basis, so only 12,863 fans showed up that day, sitting in clumps along the sidelines with the majority of the stands left empty. They got a double-header for their money, watching the USC freshmen defeat Santa Ana High School before Coach "Gloomy Gus" Henderson and his Trojans christened their new home with a 23–7 victory over Pomona.

Fight On!

Before Milo Sweet began studying dentistry at USC, he had something of a history in vaudeville. So when the university held a spirit contest in 1922, the young student called upon his musical background to write a tune. He added lyrics with the help of colleague Glen Grant. The result? One of the best-known fight songs in all of college sports.

> *Fight On for ol' SC*
> *Our men Fight On to victory.*
> *Our Alma Mater dear,*
> *Looks up to you*
> *Fight On and win*
> *For ol' SC*
> *Fight On to victory*
> *Fight On!*

"Fight On" has been a mainstay at USC games for more than 80 years, an upbeat melody of tubas, trumpets, and saxophones that has made its way into numerous recordings and films. According to one story, it blared from loudspeakers on the deck of a World War II troop transport as American soldiers stormed a Pacific island held by the Japanese. The men reportedly let out a roar.

Not bad for a guy who ultimately made his living as an orthodontist, but Sweet's tale is not the only oddity involving USC and athletic fanfare. About the same time, another student named Al Wesson wrote the school's alma mater, "All Hail." A journalism major and self-proclaimed "world's worst trumpet player" in the marching band, Wesson contributed a number of songs to a student fundraiser called "Campus Frolics of 1923." Among the frivolous tunes, he thought it would be "a good idea to wind up with something more stately and serious," something to reflect that students "really did love" their school. The music reportedly came to him while he was riding on a streetcar toward downtown Los Angeles.

USC already had an alma mater, the "University Hymn," which dated back to the early 1900s. But one of Wesson's classmates began playing "All Hail" at the end of chapel hour, and the melody caught on. It is now performed after every football game, with fans and players alike swaying to its graceful tempo, singing, "Loud let thy praises ring." As for Wesson, he would later serve for many years as the school's sports information director.

There are no such unusual tales surrounding USC's other familiar tune, "Conquest." The victory march was composed by Alfred Newman for the 1947 film *Captain from Castile* and eventually adopted by the university.

Al Wesson stands beside famed football coach Howard Jones in 1933. Ten years earlier, as a student, Wesson wrote "All Hail" for a campus show. The song became the school's alma mater.

TROJAN TRIUMPHS

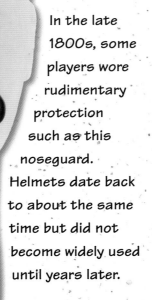

In the late 1800s, some players wore rudimentary protection such as this noseguard. Helmets date back to about the same time but did not become widely used until years later.

The Coliseum opened in 1923 with rows of bench seats that accommodated 76,000 people. The stadium was only one-sixth filled for USC's inaugural home game against Pomona.

The earliest football shoes had leather cleats affixed to their soles. On rainy days, teams had to take their shoes to a cobbler, who would put on longer cleats for the muddy fields.

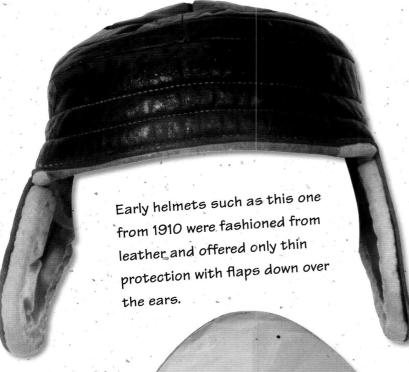

Early helmets such as this one from 1910 were fashioned from leather and offered only thin protection with flaps down over the ears.

The 1918 coaching staff. Dean Cromwell, second from right, is most famous for coaching the track team for 39 years. He is known as the "Maker of Champions."

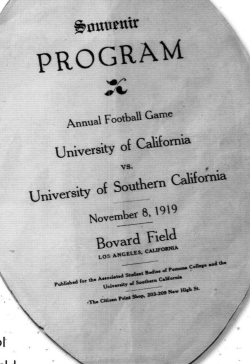

This program is from USC's 1919 game against California. In the years before the Coliseum was built, the Trojans played many of their games on school grounds at Bovard Field.

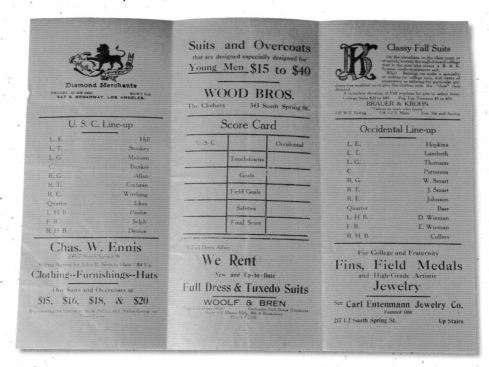

In the old days, players stayed on the field for offense and defense, as can be seen in the lineups for this 1909 game between USC and Occidental.

The Granddaddy of Them All

The Trojans make their Rose Bowl debut with a hard-fought 14–3 victory over Penn State on New Year's Day 1923.

Forty-three thousand fans had taken their seats, and the Trojans were ready to play. The Rose Bowl, on January 1, 1923, lacked only one thing—an opponent. Penn State was nowhere to be found. When the Nittany Lions finally arrived, USC coach "Gloomy Gus" Henderson accused them of stalling and an argument erupted.

Though Penn State had merely been caught in traffic, the Trojans seemed unsettled, committing a costly penalty and struggling to stop the run early on. Penn State quarterback Mike Palm drove his team downfield, sending a 20-yard drop kick through the uprights for a 3–0 lead. Minutes later, USC squandered an opportunity by fumbling just short of the end zone.

College football was nothing new to Pasadena. The Tournament of Roses first hosted an "East-West" game in 1902 and, after a hiatus, resumed its New Year's Day tradition in 1916. With a new stadium in the Arroyo Seco, the 1923 game was the first Rose Bowl played there. On such an auspicious occasion, USC wasn't giving up without a fight.

The Trojan defense sparked a turnaround in the second quarter, shutting down the run and exposing Penn State's anemic passing game. The offense soon took over as fullback Harold Galloway caught a pass flat on his back at the 2-yard line, setting up a short touchdown by Tank Campbell. Halfback Roy "Bullet" Baker added another touchdown in the third quarter to make the final score 14–3. "It is my personal belief that USC should have won by about four more touchdowns," Henderson told the *Los Angeles Times*.

Because of the late kickoff, the game ended in darkness. As the *Times* described it: "Hundreds of cigars being lighted gave the impression of hundreds of fireflies flitting about the stadium." Little did anyone know that USC's victory was the first of many Rose Bowl triumphs to come.

Harsh Words

The 1923 Rose Bowl was, by all accounts, a game of big hits and bruising tackles. But the action on the field was nothing compared to the angry words traded between the coaches before kickoff. USC's bespectacled "Gloomy Gus" Henderson became incensed when Penn State arrived late, suspicious of a psychological ploy. Nittany Lion coach Hugo Bezdek blamed traffic, and a shouting match ensued. Some news reports had fists flying; others said the pair was separated.

"The best team won," Henderson said afterward. "Good coaching, like the effect of cigarettes, always tells in the long run."

Bezdek shot back: "USC was lucky… when going at its best, my team could beat USC by forty points."

As for the pregame scuffle, the Penn State coach added: "My only wish is that Elmer Henderson had left his glasses at home."

The Early Stars

Tank Campbell and Turk Hunter. Indian Newman and Hayden Phythian. Butter Gorrell and Rabbit Malette. The pioneering days of USC football were made all the more colorful by the young men who played the game.

Early on, the Trojans came by stars in haphazard fashion, culling whatever talent they could find on campus. But when "Gloomy Gus" Henderson took over as coach, his tireless recruiting brought the likes of Chet Dolley, Harold Galloway, and Leo Calland to the program and, by the early 1920s, the speedy pair of Hobo Kincaid and Roy "Bullet" Baker were running circles around the opposition, leading USC to national prominence.

Henderson is also credited with signing future All-Americans Brice Taylor, Mort Kaer, and Morley Drury, the Hall of Fame quarterback who became known as "The Noblest Trojan of Them All." Taylor and Kaer played as sophomores for Henderson in 1924, but by the time they were truly wreaking havoc on the field, their coach had been fired.

Maybe the best of all the early players was a young man who ended up breaking his team's heart. Dan McMillan grew up in Los Angeles, attending Manual Arts High School before enrolling at the university in 1917. Playing along the line, he quickly proved to be a fierce blocker and tackler as the Trojans put together a winning record and fought rival California in a scoreless game.

After his second season, McMillan enlisted as a pilot for the United States in World War I.

In flight school near Berkeley, he befriended several Cal players and was so impressed with what they said about their school that he decided to transfer after the war. The Golden Bears were in the midst of a historic era, with coach Andy Smith leading his "Wonder Teams" to a 50-game unbeaten streak that included four consecutive victories over USC. Playing beside Harold "Brick" Muller in the trenches, McMillan received All-America mention from Walter Camp in 1920, then made consensus All-American in 1921, helping Cal to its second consecutive Rose Bowl appearance.

At the end of his college days, the future Hall of Fame lineman claimed never to have forgotten his old school. In one of his final games, he recovered a USC fumble and nearly returned it for a touchdown in what he called the "biggest thrill" of his career.

Speedy halfback Roy "Bullet" Baker (above) starred in the early 1920s. Hobo Kincaid (left) is from the same era.

The Trojans Come of Age

1925–1950

A determined new coach arrives on campus in the spring of 1925, and everything changes for USC football. Howard Jones ushers the Trojans into a golden era filled with All-Americans, Rose Bowls, and national championships. And a few movie stars, too.

Near left: *On the field, Al Krueger provides the heroics for the Trojans, hauling in this 19-yard touchdown pass from Doyle Nave to beat Duke 7–3.* **Far left:** *Child star Shirley Temple graces the cover of the 1939 Tournament of Roses program.*

USC quarterback Homer Griffith flips head-over-heels for a touchdown against California in this 1932 game won by the Trojans 27–7.

The Headman

Former Yale star Howard Jones proved he could coach the game by making USC a powerhouse.

After the 1924 season and the departure of Elmer "Gloomy Gus" Henderson, the Trojans went looking for a new coach. Not just any coach: They wanted Knute Rockne. The Notre Dame icon, in the middle of a historic career with the Fighting Irish, visited Southern California for a football seminar and by some accounts, considered switching schools at the urging of his wife. He was talked out of it upon returning to South Bend.

So the Trojans turned instead to a former star end from Yale named Howard Jones. What Jones might have lacked in name recognition he made up for with utter determination. In an era of two-way players, a time before face masks, he favored a blunt attack from the single-wing formation with his quarterback deep in the backfield, a precursor to the modern tailback. While an occasional pass or wingback reverse found its way into the game plan, such was Jones's determination to pound

the ball downfield that his teams became known as the "Thundering Herd."

This hard-nosed approach produced instant results, the Trojans going 11–2 in his first season. Jones would amass a 121–36–13 record over 16 seasons, winning five Rose Bowls and four national championships, two of those titles during a 27-game undefeated streak that spanned from 1931 to 1933. His success was all the more remarkable because he favored quality competition, gradually dropping the likes of Pomona and Cal Tech from the schedule, and replacing them with national opponents such as Colorado and Georgia. In 1926, he established the intersectional rivalry with Notre Dame—a chance to match wits with Rockne—and the annual game soon took its place among the great traditions in college football.

Though not much of a recruiter, Jones coached 20 All-Americans, including ball carriers Morley Drury, Mort Kaer, and Cotton Warburton, a talented blocking back in Erny Pinckert, and tough linemen such as Nate Barragar, Tay Brown, and Aaron Rosenberg. USC's rugged style of play required a deep bench; the coach often sent an

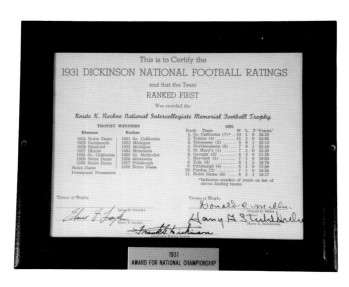

The Dickinson System, one of several polls in the early days of college football, named USC its top team in 1931.

entirely new lineup into the game to begin the second half. "One was just as good as the other," former lineman Carl Benson said. "In fact, the team that didn't start usually scored more."

But Jones's legacy extended beyond winning records and postseason honors. To players, he became known as "The Headman," a nearly mythic figure. An intellectual. A defensive tactician. A stickler for detail. Former quarterback Ambrose "Amby" Schindler recalls a game against Notre Dame in which a Trojan defender lined up "six inches wider than Howard Jones wanted him. The runner broke inside and went 60 yards for a touchdown. That's how exact the coach was... and we had to do things his way or we didn't play."

Though his teams were devoted to him, Jones rarely returned the affection. "Not the kind of guy who shot the breeze or anything," Benson said. "You wouldn't stop him on the street to talk and, if you did, he probably wouldn't talk to you." Utterly focused on his job, he lost keys, drove through red lights, and forgot more than a few appointments. One oft-told story had his assistants helping him find his car in the parking lot at the end of each day. "Everything was football," Schindler said. "All his thoughts were about football."

In the summer of 1941, Jones was looking to rebound from a disappointing season, excited about the talent returning to his team, when he suffered a fatal heart attack. He was 55 years old. USC had lost perhaps its greatest coach ever.

Players gather around coach Howard Jones at this practice during the 1937 season.

Hall of Fame

When the College Football Hall of Fame inducted its inaugural class in 1951, officials went looking for legends. Jim Thorpe, Red Grange, Knute Rockne, Amos Alonzo Stagg. And Howard Jones. Voters considered more than just Jones's tenure at USC. He was a standout athlete for Yale in the early 1900s and subsequently became the Elis' first paid coach, for a reported annual salary of $2,500. Next came stops at a variety of schools, including Ohio State and Iowa, before he landed in Los Angeles. Citing his "rarely matched" sense of sportsmanship, the Hall of Fame notes: "Moments before a USC–Stanford game, Jones visited the Stanford locker room and discovered Cardinal All-American halfback Bobby Grayson was nursing an injured knee. Jones returned to the USC quarters and instructed his players to avoid hitting Grayson in the crippled leg. They never did."

The First All-American

Born without a left hand, Brice Taylor used his natural speed, endurance, and aggressive tackling on defense to become a star at USC and the school's first All-American.

It was fairly obvious that Brice Taylor faced challenges. He stood among the smaller players on a line that featured several starters above the 200-pound mark. He was black in an era before most college football teams were integrated. And looking at photographs of the square-jawed young man, you can see that he was born without a left hand. But for all the obstacles set before him, Taylor was also USC's first All-American.

Speed was key to his success. This descendant of the Native American chief Tecumseh could run the 100-yard dash in ten seconds flat. That made him a perfect leader for coach Howard Jones's "Thundering Herd," charging ahead of ball carriers as a guard, throwing vicious blocks. On defense, Jones put him at the tackle spot so he could race around the field deflecting passes, chasing down ball carriers, and otherwise disrupting the opponent's offense. As the *Los Angeles Times* wrote: "His tackling was deadly."

In the three seasons Taylor was in the lineup, the Trojans went 28–6 and won the 1924 Christmas Festival game against Missouri. Still, his career was not without tribulation. After being named All-American as a junior in 1925—and running on USC's world-record mile relay team—he skipped spring football practice to work as a car salesman to support his wife and baby. Jones set about grooming a younger player to take his place as the *Times* reported on grumblings that perhaps "the morale of the team would be better if Taylor did not play." The senior remained unconcerned, telling a reporter: "Football doesn't start until September. I'll be out with the rest of them then, doing my level best to hold down the guard position, which has been my spot during the past two years."

That final season began with Taylor on the bench, but he quickly won back the starting job, in large part because of his durability. He rarely left the game to rest for even a minute. The Trojans suffered a pair of heartbreaking losses to Stanford and Notre Dame in 1926, but their small, fleet lineman finished his career in suitable fashion. After college, he worked as a pastor and football coach, a teacher for the Los Angeles school district, and president of small Guadalupe College in Texas.

The Duke

So many talented athletes played along the USC line in the mid-1920s—Brice Taylor, Butter Gorrell, and Jeff Cravath, among others—it was easy for a right tackle to get lost in the shuffle. Marion Morrison never garnered much attention as a reserve on the bench. His fame came years later, after he changed his name to John Wayne.

Morrison played for the Trojans in 1925 and '26 but saw his football days end abruptly with a shoulder injury that, according to news reports, occurred either in practice, during a Notre Dame game, or surfing to impress sorority girls at Balboa Beach. As one career ended, another began.

In those days, it was common for USC players to get jobs at Hollywood studios. Morrison worked as a prop man and struck up a friendship with director John Ford. Under his newly adopted stage name, he acted in a string of bit parts before making his first feature film, *Men Without Women*, in 1930. Then, in 1939, Ford cast him in *Stagecoach*, launching a career that would eventually include *Red River* and an Academy Award–winning performance in *True Grit*.

As the years passed, Wayne joked about Hollywood publicity blurbs that exaggerated his athletic prowess, telling the venerable columnist Jim Murray, "I was the only guy who ever made the 1930 All-American team in 1960. I was the unanimous choice of the Hollywood Publicists Guild."

The actor known as "The Duke" remained proud of his football heritage; he was a fan of the Trojans and coach John McKay. He sent notes of encouragement to the team and, at least once, spoke to players before a big game. "I did play for Howard Jones's Trojans," he told Murray. "Coach Jones always spoke highly of me. What he did was scream at me."

Many Trojan players have traded football for the movies, including a reserve lineman who became the Western icon John Wayne.

Casting Call

Cotton Warburton, a USC star in the 1930s, focuses his camera on Bette Davis.

When it comes to USC football players going Hollywood, John Wayne is the best-known example, but he's not the only one. The connection dates back to the 1920s and scandalous—if unsubstantiated—rumors about actress Clara Bow consorting with players. In the years that followed, quarterback Nick Pappas served as Pat O'Brien's double in *Knute Rockne All-American* and tackle Ward Bond starred in the television series *Wagon Train.* O. J. Simpson appeared in commercials and films, including *The Naked Gun.* Patrick Muldoon, a walk-on tight end from the 1980s, was in *Melrose Place* and the soap opera *Days of Our Lives.* Other Trojans had successful careers behind the camera. Aaron Rosenberg, a two-time All-American guard in the early 1930s, produced dozens of films, and Cotton Warburton, an All-America back from the same era, won an Oscar for film editing on *Mary Poppins.*

"Good Enough to Win"

Don Williams, a quarterback who could move the ball through the air and on the ground, led a USC team loaded with present and future All-Americans to a 9–0–1 record and a national championship in 1928.

Halfway through the 1928 season, USC had the looks of a very good team, maybe a great one. The Trojans had plowed through a handful of lesser opponents and battled California to a 0–0 tie in Berkeley. The real test came when legendary coach Pop Warner brought Stanford to the Coliseum in early November. The Cardinals—as they were known then—had not lost to the Trojans in three years. But this time USC coach Howard Jones, ever the tactician, had a trick up his sleeve.

Stanford was bigger along the line of scrimmage by ten pounds per man, so Jones employed an early version of the blitz called the "quick mix," attacking the opposing offense, disrupting any sense of rhythm, and forcing seven turnovers. The result? A 10–0 victory before 80,000 fans that catapulted the Trojans toward their first national championship. "We went into the game to do our best, and our best was good enough to win," tackle Jesse Hibbs told reporters. "I'm the happiest guy in the world, I guess, for our victory today."

The Trojans had established themselves as a West Coast power, a reputation they burnished the next week in a 78–7 blowout win over Arizona. This USC squad was loaded with All-Americans present and future. Quarterback Don Williams led the team in rushing and could throw the ball. Francis Tappaan played end and Nate Barragar anchored the line at center. With the offense hitting on all cylinders, Hibbs led a defense that would surrender just 59 points all season.

As winter approached, Pacific Coast Conference foes Washington State and Idaho fell by the wayside. The regular-season finale saw more than 72,000 fans pack the Coliseum as the Trojans earned their first victory in the fledgling intersectional rivalry with Notre Dame, sailing to a 27–14 victory behind Williams's 111 yards and two touchdowns. USC finished with a 9–0–1 record.

Tense relations between university administrators and Rose Bowl officials—the Trojans were convinced the Tournament of Roses did not like them—prompted the team to decline an invitation to the New Year's Day game. It turned out they didn't need to play in Pasadena. The highly respected Dickinson System cited strength of schedule in placing the "Thundering Herd" ahead of Cal and Georgia Tech as the No. 1 team in the land.

The USC defense stops Notre Dame on this play from the 1928 game, the Trojans' first victory over the Irish in their budding rivalry.

The Rivals

For all the big games that USC played during the Howard Jones era—the battles with established powers California and Stanford, the Rose Bowl victories—none turned out to be more important than the Saturday afternoons when the Trojans squared off against Notre Dame and UCLA. From those early meetings, two lasting rivalries were born.

Much debate has focused on the origin of the Notre Dame game. The most popular story has USC graduate manager Gwynn Wilson meeting with Irish coach Knute Rockne on a train to pitch the idea. While Wilson argued unsuccessfully, his wife sat in an adjacent compartment discussing sunny Southern California with Rockne's wife. Legend has it that Bonnie Rockne, eager to spend time in Los Angeles, persuaded her husband to take the game.

A simpler, less quaint theory has the rivalry arising from a desire by both schools to generate ticket revenue. Their first meeting in 1926 drew a sold-out crowd to the Coliseum. The next fall, the game was held at Soldier Field in Chicago and a record 120,000 fans watched a thrilling 7–6 Notre Dame victory. Either way, a grand tradition had taken hold. As former Irish running back Jerome Bettis said: "Some of the other games you played, you might not remember. USC games—you remember everything."

The Substitute

At the Coliseum, the Trojans had built a 12–7 lead and were only a few minutes from winning the first-ever game against Notre Dame on December 4, 1926. That's when the legendary coach of the Irish, Knute Rockne, pulled a rabbit out of his hat.

Calling star quarterback Charles Riley off the field, Rockne sent in a little-known reserve, a skinny kid named Art Parisien. With whispers still filtering through the curious crowd, the left-hander rolled out and completed a 35-yard pass to Johnny Niemiec. Jeff Cravath, the USC team captain and a stalwart on defense all day, made a touchdown-saving tackle at the 20-yard line, but Parisien was just getting started.

A couple of plays later, the substitute threw to Niemiec again and this time Cravath arrived too late. The Irish players piled on each other in the end zone, celebrating a 13–12 victory.

While the Trojans got off to a rousing start with the team from South Bend, the same could not be said for their other rivalry. USC had been around almost four decades before the UCLA campus opened, and it wasn't until 1929 that the Bruins felt confident enough to propose a meeting on the football field. The first two games drew big crowds, but the Trojans won by lopsided scores of 76–0 and 52–0. UCLA took a six-year break before returning in 1936 with a team strong enough to earn a 7–7 tie to truly ignite the crosstown feud.

Top: *A Notre Dame–USC game program from 1932.* **Above:** *Quarterback Morley Drury breaks through the line in this game against Notre Dame at Soldier Field in 1927.*

PIGSKIN REVIEW
1938
SOUTHERN CALIFORNIA vs. CALIFORNIA

S.146 Selling Price
.004 Sales Tax
Total Price **25 cents**

An official program from USC's 13–7 upset win over third-ranked California at the Coliseum in 1938.

A helmet autographed by Al Krueger, the second-string end who secured a place in Trojan history by scoring against Duke in the 1939 Rose Bowl.

The "Thundering Herd" of 1931 snuck past Notre Dame in the final minute and went on to win a national championship. The plaque on this photo proclaims their dominance.

Tickets from the 1938 USC–UCLA game advise male students to wear white shirts and sit in one section and female students to sit in another.

USC coach Howard Jones glowers from the cover of Time magazine in November 1932, his team on its way to a second straight national title.

Gaius "Gus" Shaver wore this bowler hat in 1931. Each player on the USC team bought a bowler to wear on the train home after the win in South Bend.

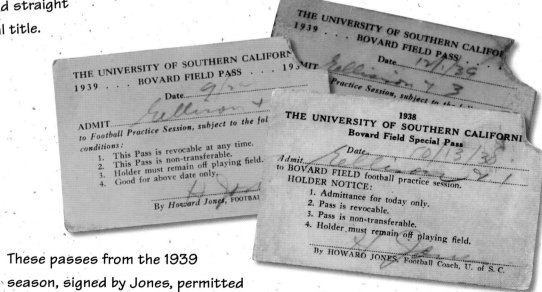

These passes from the 1939 season, signed by Jones, permitted the bearer to watch the team practice on Bovard Field.

A Run for the Ages

The Trojans' 21–12 win over unbeaten Tulane in the 1932 Rose Bowl was but one of the highlights in a winning streak that spanned three seasons.

The 1931 season did not begin well. Playing at home against underdog St. Mary's, the Trojans wasted early opportunities and surrendered two touchdown passes in the third quarter. The 13–7 upset appeared to ruin USC's season, but St. Mary's coach Slip Madigan warned fans not to be fooled, telling the *Los Angeles Times:* "I think Southern California will go a long ways this year." He was right.

The Trojans rebounded to whip Oregon State 30–0 the next week, launching an undefeated streak that spanned 27 games over three seasons, including two national championships. They were led by a string of All-Americans, big linemen such as Tay Brown leading the way for halfback Erny Pinckert and quick-footed quarterback Cotton Warburton. Still, left end Julie Bescos recalled, "No one said 'I'm a big shot.' We were a team all the way through."

USC plowed through the Pacific Coast Conference in 1931 with wins over Oregon, California, and Stanford.

The team then traveled to Notre Dame, where Johnny Baker kicked a 33-yard field goal with one minute remaining to give the Trojans a 16–14 victory, their first in South Bend. The season ended with a 21–12 win over undefeated Tulane in the Rose Bowl. Bernie Bierman, the famed Tulane coach, said: "Southern California's Trojans have more power than any team I have ever seen."

The following season was even better. They rolled over Stanford and Oregon and beat Notre Dame on homecoming. They escaped close calls, scoring in the final minutes against Loyola and slipping to a 9–6 victory at muddy Washington. In the Rose Bowl, Warburton led the way past Pittsburgh, 35–0, to seal a 10–0 record and a second consecutive national title.

The unbeaten streak ended in 1933 when USC ran up against Stanford's "Vow Boys," players who made a pact never to lose to the Trojans. The 13–7 defeat ended hopes for another trip to the Rose Bowl and a third crown, but it could not dim the legacy.

The Substitute, Part II

The Trojans featured a pair of present and future All-Americans on offense, but the Duke Blue Devils owned a perfect record and a defense that had yet to surrender a point. The 1939 Rose Bowl figured to be a low-scoring affair.

Duke's fourth-quarter field goal gave them a seemingly insurmountable 3–0 lead. USC coach Howard Jones summoned a bit of magic, copying a Notre Dame ploy used against his team a decade earlier.

Jones replaced Grenny Lansdell with reserve Doyle Nave. The fourth-string quarterback drove USC into Duke territory, completing three straight passes to Al Krueger, a second-stringer himself. As the clock ticked down to 40 seconds, Nave spotted Krueger open. The pass was perfect, and the 19-yard touchdown gave USC a come-from-behind 7–3 victory.

Meet You at Tommy

When USC reached its 50th anniversary in 1930, university administrators wanted to celebrate with something memorable. They paid Roger Noble Burnham $10,000 to create a statue exemplifying the school's fighting spirit. That was a considerable sum of money in those days, large enough that the university placed a $1 surcharge on football season tickets.

Burnham looked to halfback Erny Pinckert, fullback Russ Saunders, and other players as inspiration for a Trojan warrior. "Burnham made more then 100 oil paintings of various football players from our squad, and from them he selected the paintings of Pinckert and me," Saunders recalled. "We put in a lot of hours posing, and the result you see is my head, chest, and shoulders. The rest is Erny."

The base of the statue bears the university seal with the Latin motto *Palmam qui meruit ferat* ("Let him who deserves it bear away the palm"). "Faithful, Scholarly, Skillful, Courageous and Ambitious" are inscribed below. Over the years, "Tommy Trojan" has served as a meeting place on campus and a target for countless pranks. USC students have stolen his sword so many times that the university uses a wooden replacement. Each year before the UCLA game, workers wrap him in plastic lest he be drenched in blue and gold paint, an annual bit of mischief that makes sense given the history of yet another school icon.

The Victory Bell started off in possession of UCLA, whose cheerleaders rang it after every touchdown. In 1941, a group of USC frat brothers infiltrated the Bruin rooting section and, afterward, helped load the bell onto a truck bound for Westwood. They also absconded with the keys. When UCLA students went looking for the replacements, the fraternity brothers drove off. The bell remained hidden for more than a year, setting off a war of pranks that escalated to the point that USC President Rufus B. von KleinSmid threatened to cancel the annual game. In 1942, the respective student body presidents met beside Tommy Trojan to sign an agreement—USC paid for half the bell, which now sits in storage all year and is presented to whichever team wins.

The Victory Bell goes to the winner of the crosstown rivalry between USC and UCLA. USC students hold the bell in 1949, because the Trojans beat UCLA 12–7.

A Second Home

In the years after USC defeated Penn State in the inaugural 1923 Rose Bowl, the Trojans had found a new home—at least on New Year's Day. Over the next three decades, they amassed a perfect record in Pasadena's annual game.

1923	USC 14, Penn State 3
1930	USC 47, Pittsburgh 14
1932	USC 21, Tulane 12
1933	USC 35, Pittsburgh 0
1939	USC 7, Duke 3
1940	USC 14, Tennessee 0
1944	USC 29, Washington 0
1945	USC 25, Tennessee 0

No other school matched USC's eight victories in those early years. The Trojans had made a good start toward becoming one of the winningest bowl teams in college football history.

Tommy Trojan, commissioned by school officials in 1930, has became a campus icon.

A Championship Delayed

The 1939 Trojans finished undefeated with a Rose Bowl victory to their credit but still had to wait more than six decades before the university officially added their names to the roster of teams that had captured national titles.

A yearbook photograph of the 1939 team shows rows of young faces, clean white jerseys, hair combed back. Football was different then, the ball fatter and rounder, helmets made of leather with no face masks. "Amby" Schindler, the quarterback, recalled: "Most guys along the line had real beat-up faces. We called Charley Morrill 'Hamburger Puss' because he was all scars."

Scholarships paid only for tuition, forcing players to work campus jobs to earn money for food, books, and lab fees. They practiced hard to make the 35-man travel squad, which allowed them to eat at a daily training table.

So the 1939 Trojans played mostly to uphold their team's proud tradition. They started slow, a 7–7 tie against Oregon, but climbed the polls by winning the next seven games—including a victory in South Bend—by a combined score of 160–26. The defense dominated as coach Howard Jones opened up the offense for his three quarterbacks: Schindler, Grenny Lansdell, and Rose Bowl hero Doyle Nave. The regular season ended with undefeated

UCLA and 103,303 fans at the Coliseum, where USC stopped the Bruins at the goal line to preserve a 0–0 tie and earn a trip to Pasadena. Schindler had missed the previous year's victory over Duke and was desperate to play on New Year's Day. When the game finally came around, halfback Joe Shell recalled, "Amby just went crazy."

USC faced the Tennessee Volunteers, who had a 23-game winning streak and had not been scored upon. Schindler played the role of spoiler, running for one touchdown and passing to "Antelope" Al Krueger for another, giving the Trojans a 14–0 win. But with the victory secure, there remained one more score to settle.

Myriad polls ranked college teams then. Texas A&M stood at No. 1 on several lists and Cornell topped another. The 8–0–2 Trojans won the Dickinson System, so the players counted themselves national champions. The university did not agree. It took more than 60 years of lobbying—until 2004—before USC added 1939 to its title banners. "It's all been given back to us," Schindler said.

A Good Friend

The shocking news: Howard Jones had died suddenly of a heart attack. The man who led USC to five Rose Bowl victories and four national championships was gone; barely a month before training camp the team needed a coach. University administrators turned to Sam Barry.

The Wisconsin native was a familiar face around campus, a longtime assistant on the team, beloved by players. "He was a sweetheart . . . like a father to me," said Julie Bescos, who played for and later coached with Barry. "He could be firm, but he was an Irishman and he had a great sense of humor." Just as important, he had been close with Jones—they were bridge partners off the field—and vowed to preserve what "The Headman" had created.

The 1941 season began with a sense of hope and a last-second victory over Oregon State, but the following week Ohio State rocked the Trojans 33–0, and things quickly turned south. The roster grew thinner, depleted by everything from injured knees to influenza, as the losses began to mount. Barry talked about his team's substandard blocking and tackling, and he suggested the situation might improve if only he could get a few more healthy bodies back on the field.

The final weeks of the season offered a few bright spots. First, the Trojans played valiantly before falling to fourth-ranked Notre Dame and its star quarterback, Angelo Bertelli, in South Bend. They came from behind to tie UCLA before a crowd of 65,000 at the Coliseum. But these moral victories could not lessen the sting of a 2–6–1 record, USC's worst showing in four decades. President Rufus B. von KleinSmid insisted that Barry could keep his job for "a long time" even as reports had the university quietly looking for a replacement. History soon intervened.

The day after the UCLA tie, Barry and his staff were driving to Palm Springs for a Pacific Coast Conference meeting when a bulletin came over the radio: The Japanese had bombed Pearl Harbor. "Oh my God," Barry said. With America rushing into World War II, he enlisted in the navy and was assigned to establish a physical fitness program for aviators at St. Mary's College. Once again, the Trojans needed a coach.

Sam Barry looks over a diagrammed play during the 1941 season. A good friend of Howard Jones, Barry took over as USC's coach after Jones suffered a fatal heart attack, but he saw his tenure cut short by the start of World War II.

A Lineman Comes Home

There wasn't anything fancy about Newell Cravath, the guy that everyone called "Jeff." Teammates say he was down-to-earth, and he liked to fish. They also said it was no surprise when USC hired him in 1942 to coach the team. The man knew football.

Cravath arrived on campus in the mid-1920s from Santa Ana High School and became a hard-hitting center for coach Howard Jones and the "Thundering Herd." After graduation, he became an assistant, working with linemen. In early 1941, shortly before Jones died, Cravath took the head-coaching job at the University of San Francisco, where he fashioned the highest-scoring offense on the West Coast. The following year, USC lured him back at a reported annual salary of $7,000.

Students gather for an animated rally around Tommy Trojan, voicing their support for embattled coach Jeff Cravath. Ultimately, it wasn't enough to save his job.

His first season was not memorable, the Trojans finishing 5–5–1. But the following spring, Cravath began hinting at big changes. Out went Jones's single-wing and spread offenses in favor of a scheme that had been successful at eastern schools. The T formation aligned three runners in a row across the backfield, giving quarterback Jim Hardy numerous options to run, throw, or hand off on each snap.

The results were immediate, the Trojans drubbing UCLA 20–0 in the 1943 opener, the start of a run that saw them post winning records for seven straight seasons and make the Rose Bowl four times. Cravath's success came when many football programs struggled or temporarily shut down, their rosters depleted by the war. Yet his victories placated neither alumni nor players who complained that he was too tough. There were stories of Cravath working his team hard before a disheartening 49–0 loss to Michigan in the 1948 Rose Bowl. The rumblings built, bringing his days at USC to an abrupt, tumultuous end.

One Losing Season

A 54–28–8 record. Four Rose Bowls. At most universities, a football coach could keep his job with those numbers. Not at USC.

For Jeff Cravath, the problems began with Rose Bowl defeats to Alabama and Michigan. The Trojans had never lost on New Year's Day, and the alumni did not like it one bit. Students held an impromptu rally at Tommy Trojan to support their coach—he walked out to thank them—

but after the team finished 2–5–2 in 1950, the only losing record in Cravath's nine seasons, he was forced to resign.

University President Fred Fagg Jr. issued a statement: "You have done much for Trojan football. . . . you have a host of friends throughout the country who will long remember your impressive record of victories at 'SC."

Cravath led USC to four Rose Bowl games.

Life During Wartime

World War II brought tremendous change to the college football landscape as vast numbers of male students left school to enlist. The National Collegiate Athletic Association tried to help by relaxing its rules, allowing freshmen to join the varsity roster for the first time, but the sudden drain on manpower forced some schools to suspend their football programs. It was a different story at USC.

While the Trojans lost several key players and even an athletic director to the war, the team benefited in other ways, as the navy and marines established training programs on campus, shipping in approximately 2,000 men. Some had been star athletes at other schools. "They were there for 18 months, so they got to play for one or two seasons," former USC assistant Julie Bescos said. "That's what saved the team."

With plenty of talent surrounding quarterback Jim Hardy, the Trojans sailed through an odd schedule in 1943, wartime travel restrictions forcing them to play UCLA and California twice each. They won the conference title and defeated Washington in the only Rose Bowl between West Coast teams. The winning continued through 1944 and another visit to Pasadena on New Year's Day. This time, undefeated USC faced a similarly perfect Tennessee, but Hardy passed for two touchdowns and ran for a third to fuel a 25–0 victory.

But if the military giveth, it also taketh away. The next fall, a number of star players—including halfback Gordon Gray and All-America tackle John Ferraro—were called

An official game program from the 1945 season.

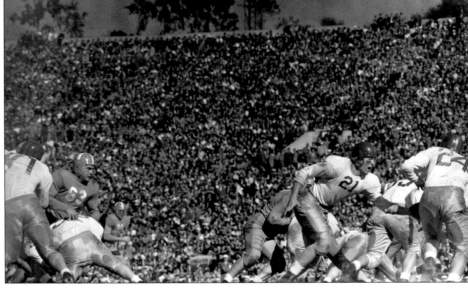

Quarterback Jim Hardy (21) hands off during the 1945 Rose Bowl. The Trojans won handily, 25–0, against a Tennessee squad that relied on freshmen during wartime.

away to serve. The Trojans lost three times during the regular season, including an upset at the hands of the San Diego navy team, and they took a heavily diluted squad to the 1946 Rose Bowl. Second-ranked Alabama blew past them by a score of 34–14, marking the first postseason defeat in school history.

Those three consecutive Rose Bowls and a 23–6–2 wartime record left fans expecting even greater things. After all, veteran players were returning from Europe and the Pacific, enhancing a roster that already featured experienced sophomores and military trainees. Yet the Trojans failed to profit from their newfound wealth. With the 1946 schedule expanded to include intersectional foes Ohio State and Notre Dame, the team stumbled to a 6–4 finish.

Ernie Smith was one of the top tackles of his era. He played on national championship teams in 1931 and 1932. This picture is of the 1932 team.

In the space of one fateful season, senior Frank Gifford went from an overlooked player to an All-America halfback. He was later inducted into the College Football Hall of Fame.

This college football board game, with a picture of Howard Jones on the box, is a much-treasured commodity among sports memorabilia collectors.

A ticket to the 1946 Rose Bowl game between USC and Alabama. Unfortunately, it was the first USC loss in nine appearances at the Rose Bowl.

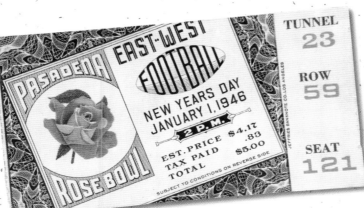

This cartoonish game program shows "Smoky Mountain boys" rushing in from Tennessee to see their team in the Rose Bowl.

This game-worn jersey is signed by right end Paul Cleary, a consensus All-American in 1947 who went on to a brief professional career.

The Trojans make front-page news in the fall of 1931, returning home to cheering crowds after a last-minute victory at Notre Dame.

The All-American Age

Erny Pinckert and Cotton Warburton (left and right, respectively) lead a quartet of former Trojans on the Pacific All-Stars team.

Harry Smith was a two-time All-American at left guard in the 1930s.

Howard Jones wasn't big on compliments. The legendary USC coach more often praised his players in subtle ways, speaking quietly after games or when their college careers ended. Former lineman Carl Benson recalls Jones approaching him after the Trojans won the 1940 Rose Bowl to earn a national championship, saying: "I think that was my best team ever."

It is difficult to pick one team or player among the All-Americans playing from 1925 to 1950. Start with Morley Drury, the quarterback known as "The Noblest Trojan of Them All." As a senior captain in 1927, he rushed for 1,163 yards, a single-season record that stood until Heisman Trophy winner Mike Garrett, four decades later.

The Trojans featured a Hall of Fame tandem in halfback Erny Pinckert and guard Johnny Baker. Pinckert was a master of deception, catching passes out of the backfield and running a pair of double-reverses for touchdowns against Tulane in the 1932 Rose Bowl. Baker was not only one of the fastest linemen in the game, he also kicked the last-minute field goal that gave USC its first victory over Notre Dame in South Bend.

The early 1930s brought a small, shifty quarterback named Irvine Warburton; teammates called him "Cotton" for his blond hair. As a schoolboy in San Diego, Warburton had been state champion in the quarter-mile. He kept his running ways at USC, once rushing for 221 yards against Washington State. Like Pinckert, he had able linemen in Aaron Rosenberg and Tay Brown, who set a Coliseum record by blocking four kicks in a game.

The next big star got his inspiration as a boy going to the movies, watching a newsreel of Baker's historic field goal. Harry Smith made it his goal to play for USC, and by the late 1930s, the guard known as "Blackjack" found himself leading the national championship team that Jones called his greatest ever. The 1940s brought more All-Americans, including ends Ralph Heywood and Paul Cleary, and left tackle John Ferraro, who made his mark on Los Angeles as a longtime city councilman. Thinking back on his college days, Benson summed it up by saying: "Just so many good football players."

Paul Cleary's All-America season in 1947 got him into the College Football Hall of Fame.

Turn on the Lights

Nearly 63,000 fans had good reason to be excited as they filed into the Coliseum on that Monday in late October 1944. They had come to watch USC face Washington, two undefeated teams meeting in a rematch of the previous season's Rose Bowl. Even better, the crowd had come to witness a historic event—the Trojans' first home game at the Coliseum under the lights.

That year, with college teams facing wartime travel restrictions, Washington needed to make the most of its trip to California by scheduling two games only days apart. The Trojans had played after dark for the first time the week before, a special game against St. Mary's Pre-Flight in Fresno, and now they returned to Los Angeles for an 8:30 P.M. kickoff with the Huskies. The official program stated: "This may well be the one and only Coliseum night game in Trojan varsity football history."

Ticket sales were brisk as the pundits argued over their predictions. USC had looked a little shaky that season, suffering early ties against UCLA and California. Washington had won all of its games behind veteran quarterback Bob Zech and fullback Keith DeCourcy, but those victories came against the likes of Whitman and Willamette—hardly Pacific Coast Conference fare. Besides, people still remembered the Trojans rolling over the Huskies 29–0 in Pasadena.

The 1944 game turned out to be a replay with the Trojans striking quickly, halfback Gordon Gray returning a punt 50 yards for a touchdown in the first quarter. A few minutes later, quarterback Jim Hardy led USC back downfield and snuck over the goal line for a 12–0 lead. A Washington turnover gave Hardy the opportunity to throw a touchdown pass with seconds remaining before halftime, and the game was all but over, the Trojans on their way to a 38–7 victory.

According to news accounts, fans loved the late kickoff and replaced the usual card stunts with a different sort of trick, everyone lighting matches with the stadium lights turned off. The teams used a special ball, its tips painted white, and more than 5,000 servicemen watched from a section where the seats were free. As for the program's suggestion that this might be a one-time event, attendance was so high that night games became a regular feature of the USC schedule.

Darting through the shadows, USC and Washington play in the first night game at the Coliseum. Notice the runner with a special football; its tips were painted white for visibility.

A Gyrating Carnival

A fraternity shows off its winning float to a crowd of more than 70,000 at the 1949 homecoming game against Stanford. As college football grew in popularity after World War II, attendance rose dramatically and games became steeped in the pageantry of marching bands, dancers, and lavish halftime shows.

The popularity of college football continued to grow after World War II, as teams returned to full strength and campuses overflowed with students. At USC, the attendance at games rose to an all-time high of 723,675 for the 1947 season, including a crowd of 104,953—still a record for football at the Coliseum—that watched USC get crushed by Heisman Trophy–winning quarter-

back Johnny Lujack and Notre Dame a few weeks before Christmas.

That same season, a USC student named Tommy Walker lettered in football. Walker was hardly the best player on the field, but he would become, in some ways, the most memorable. A member of the marching band, he would tear off his band uniform once the game began,

In the late 1940s, Tommy Walker became known to USC fans for tearing off his band uniform once the game began, putting on football gear, and kicking extra points for the team. He was known as "Tommy Trojan."

run down from the stands, and kick extra points. Fellow students called him "Tommy Trojan." Walker, who directed the band after graduation and later served as head of entertainment at Disneyland, became known for one more thing. While in school, he composed the trumpet "Charge" that remains a staple at sporting events worldwide.

Newspaper accounts from that era make the Coliseum sound as if it transformed into a carnival on Saturday afternoons. At the 1949 homecoming game against Stanford, the respective bands "went through a lot of complicated gyrations on the field while 20 girls did an Indian dance, 10 floats circled the track, both rooting sections did card

stunts and an airplane dragged some advertising over 70,000-odd heads," the *Los Angeles Times* reported.

Things were changing for the players, too. Leather helmets were on their way out, and the age of the athletic scholarship was underway. The 1948 team took its first trip to an away game by airplane. On the way home from a disheartening loss to Oregon, the pilot—a USC grad—took the players over Yosemite and Crater Lake.

Dog Days at USC

Long before a majestic white horse and costumed rider galloped around the field after every USC touchdown, the Trojans had a very different mascot. George Tirebiter I was a scruffy mutt who got his nickname by habitually chasing cars across campus. Adopted by students, he began appearing at games in 1940 and, according to the university publication *SCampus*, "his wild barking and excitement [were] interpreted as a dog's way of expressing joy."

Reportedly a disagreeable animal, Tirebiter attacked California's human mascot at a 1947 game and was later dognapped by UCLA students, who shaved their school letters on his hindquarters. These incidents only added to the legend of a dog that posed with homecoming queens and once rode in a parade around the Coliseum track, drawing cheers from the crowd. His days as a mascot came to an end when he was struck by a car and killed in 1950. George II, George III, and George IV succeeded him in the following years.

George Tirebiter I, an early Trojan mascot

The McKay Years

1951–1975

After a down period in Trojan football, a new coach named John McKay guides the program toward a triumphant new era. USC becomes known as "Tailback U" with a string of gifted runners powering the team to Rose Bowl victories and national championships.

Jon Arnett wore number 26 for the Trojans and was a triple-threat player for USC. He won the Voit Award, which is given to the best player on the West Coast.

Halfback Angelo Coia stretches for an 11-yard pass from quarterback Willie Wood, scoring the Trojans' first touchdown in a hard-fought 30–28 victory over Stanford in 1959.

Anthony Davis bobbles the football on a Student Body Right against Oregon in 1972. The Trojans prevailed 18–0, taking a another step toward the national title.

The Fullback Becomes Coach

Ten years after the sudden death of Howard Jones, USC football was in many ways still trying to regain its footing. The Trojans had been through two coaches— Sam Barry and Jeff Cravath—enjoying modest success but nothing near the heights they reached with the Headman. When Cravath was forced to resign after his only losing season in 1950, the program turned to Jess Hill.

Fans might recall Jess Hill (standing beside halfback Jon Arnett) as a successful coach, leading USC to six consecutive winning seasons in the 1950s. But Hill was equally talented as a fullback for the Trojans in the 1920s, a pro baseball player, and after his coaching days, one of the top athletic directors in the nation.

An extraordinarily talented athlete in his youth, Hill played fullback for Jones in the late 1920s while also lettering in baseball and track, in which he was the first broad jumper in school history to surpass 25 feet. He then played professional baseball for a decade, which included stints with the New York Yankees and Washington Senators. USC brought him back to coach the freshman football team in 1946 and, five seasons later, handed him the reins to the varsity.

"Actually, football isn't too complicated," he told the *Los Angeles Times*. "Do you know any football coaches who are geniuses? Neither do I."

Hill immediately shifted his offense to a scheme that combined elements of the T and single wing, all the better to take advantage of an underused senior halfback named Frank Gifford. The change brought immediate improvement as USC went 7–3 with a 28–6 win over Army in Hill's old stomping grounds, Yankee Stadium, and a victory over Cal that ended the Golden Bears' 38-game regular-season undefeated streak. By 1952, Hill had the Trojans back in the Rose Bowl, where they defeated Wisconsin 7–0.

The team was on its way to six consecutive winning seasons that included yet another Rose Bowl appearance, a 20–7 loss to Ohio State in 1955, before Hill stepped down after the 1956 season. "Say, I'm getting old," the 49-year-old joked. His 45–17–1 record was successful by most standards, but any man who coached at USC still found himself languishing in Jones's shadow.

Twenty-nine Titles

When fans talk about the great coaches in USC history, Jess Hill rarely gets mentioned. But there is a reason why his bust appears beside the likes of Howard Jones and John McKay in Heritage Hall.

Before he took over the football team, Hill succeeded the legendary track coach Dean Cromwell, leading the Trojans to a pair of undefeated seasons and consecutive national championships. After football, he ran the athletic department from 1957 to 1972, overseeing several of the greatest names in coaching history: McKay, Rod Dedeaux in baseball, and George Toley in tennis.

So it was no surprise when Hill was named "Athletic Director of the Decade" in 1969. During his tenure, USC won 29 national championships in a variety of sports that included swimming and gymnastics. And, oh yes, a couple of titles in football.

"They All Came to See Us"

Trouble arose shortly after the Trojans arrived in Texas for the 1956 season opener against the Longhorns. As players milled about the lobby of the team hotel, waiting to check in, quarterback Frank Hall recalled the concierge announcing: "By the way, we've arranged to have your three Negro players stay at another hotel."

College football was still largely white in the mid-1950s; Texas was more than a decade from integrating its team. The Trojans had agreed to play in Austin on the condition that their black players—C. R. Roberts, Louis Byrd, and Hillard Hill—be allowed to participate, but apparently no one had informed the hotel. Players recall coach Jess Hill reacting immediately. "I'll tell you what," he said to the concierge, "we won't be staying here."

Team officials scrambled to find alternate accommodations, and once the team settled in at a new location, porters and maids began sneaking up to the room that Roberts shared with Byrd and Hill. "Back then, all the hotel workers were black," Roberts said. "They all came to see us. We didn't sleep a wink the whole night."

If black football players were a rarity in the Southwest, Roberts made sure that the 47,000 fans attending that late-September game took notice. With Texas leading 7–0 at the start of the second quarter, the fullback shot around the left end for a 73-yard touchdown. Several plays later, after a Longhorn fumble, he went 50 yards to give the Trojans a 13–7 lead. "He had size and sprinter's speed," teammate Jon Arnett said. "He was a little ahead of his time."

A little ahead of the Longhorn tacklers, too. In the third quarter, Roberts broke free yet again and sprinted 74 yards for his third touchdown. By evening's end, he had gained a school record 251 yards on 12 carries, leading USC to a 44–20 victory against a highly regarded opponent.

Years later, Roberts and Byrd remember that the only time they sensed anger was when Roberts tackled the Texas quarterback and they heard a rumbling from the stands. The coach pulled Roberts off defense for the rest of the game, solving that problem. Otherwise, the USC players said, the game went smoothly. And when the Trojans emerged from their locker room afterward, Hall recalled stepping into a sea of ten-gallon hats, "all those men waiting to shake C. R.'s hand."

> "He [C. R. Roberts] had size and sprinter's speed. He was a little ahead of his time."
>
> **Jon Arnett**

This is the game ball from the 1956 game against Texas, signed by USC team members.

C. R. Roberts

The Rivalry

The moment Johnny Baker's field goal sailed through the uprights on that November day in 1931, giving the Trojans their first victory at South Bend, the rivalry between USC and Notre Dame took hold. The Trojans had raised themselves to the level of the storied Irish football program, setting the stage for last-second victories and staggering upsets to come.

Not all the dramatic finishes went USC's way. In 1926, substitute quarterback Art Parisien came off the bench to throw a fourth-quarter touchdown pass, giving Notre Dame a 13–12 victory. The Irish scored with 35 seconds remaining to forge a 14–14 tie in 1948, extending their unbeaten streak to 28. But when it comes to the greatest intersectional showdown of them all, two games stand out—at least for Trojan fans.

The Irish arrived at the Coliseum in 1964 undefeated and led by quarterback John Huarte, who had won the Heisman Trophy a few days earlier. They were on the way to a comfortable win, leading 17–0, when momentum shifted in the second half. USC closed the gap to four points, then they drove to within 15 yards of the end zone as the seconds ticked away.

On fourth down, USC halfback Rod Sherman mentioned to his quarterback, Craig Fertig, that he had noticed a gap in the middle of Notre Dame's secondary. Fertig called the play: 84 Z Delay. With tailback Mike Garrett going in motion, Fertig took the snap and fired to a point where Sherman was sprinting on a slant route. "Just as I let it go, Alan Page hits me square in the face," Fertig recalled. Flat on his back, Fertig heard the crowd erupt. He wanted to sit up to see what had happened, but the Irish defensive lineman lay on top of him.

"Get up, get up," an official barked at Page.

"I can't," he replied. "We're stuck." Their facemasks had locked together.

Someone had to help untangle them; only then could Fertig celebrate his touchdown pass. The 20–17 upset ranked as USC's greatest moment against Notre Dame. Until ten years later.

The 1974 game—known forever after as "The Comeback"—began with the Irish racing to a big lead before a subdued Coliseum crowd. Though the Trojans scored just before halftime, they trailed 24–6 and their prospects

The USC–Notre Dame game has always been a hot ticket, including this one from 1955.

Tailback Mike Garrett runs for daylight in a 1964 victory over Notre Dame at the Coliseum. The annual game between the Trojans and the Irish ranks among college football's best rivalries.

looked bleak. In the locker room, coach John McKay outlined his plan for victory: "They're going to kick it to A. D.," he said, referring to star tailback Anthony Davis, "and he's going to bring it all the way back." The players figured the coach had gone crazy.

But when the second half began, Davis took the kickoff and raced 102 yards for a touchdown, igniting an offensive frenzy. In that third quarter, the tailback scored twice more and quarterback Pat Haden threw a pair of scoring passes to his favorite receiver: the coach's son, J. K. McKay. The scoring continued into the fourth quarter as Haden threw yet another touchdown pass and safety Charles Phillips returned an interception 58 yards to the end zone. As Davis put it, "We turned into madmen."

Fifty-five points in just under 17 minutes. Never before had college football witnessed a comeback so startling and explosive, and that victory is what catapulted the Trojans to a national championship. It certainly wasn't the last memorable USC–Notre Dame game—not with the 2005 "Bush Push" looming in the future—but even the Trojan players had trouble explaining what happened on the field that day.

Anthony Davis became known as "the Notre Dame Killer" for scoring 11 touchdowns in three games against the rival Irish.

"I can't understand it," J. K. McKay said afterward. "I'm gonna sit down tonight and have a beer and think about it. Against Notre Dame? Maybe against Kent State...but Notre Dame?"

"Tougher Than an Irish Skull"

The winner of the annual USC–Notre Dame game takes possession of a strange-looking trophy with an even stranger-sounding name. The Shillelagh (pronounced shuh-LAY-lee) is a reproduction of a Gaelic war club. It is about a foot long, gnarled, burnished, and covered with tiny medallions—Trojan heads and shamrocks—denoting each year's victor.

Legend has it that shillelaghs must be fashioned from saplings of oak or blackthorn because those are the only woods "tougher than an Irish skull." When the Notre Dame Alumni Club of Los Angeles created the trophy in 1952, they supposedly had it flown from Ireland by Howard Hughes's pilot. The original Shillelagh ran out of room for medallions in 1989, so it was enshrined at Notre Dame. The tradition lapsed for eight years before a new, slightly longer Shillelagh II was created in 1997.

Carson Palmer celebrates while holding Shillelagh II after USC beat Notre Dame 44–13 in 2002.

Scandal Hits the PCC

News broke in early 1956: There were reports of Washington boosters funneling cash to recruits for "transportation, entertainment, and expenses." It was the start of a scandal that swept through the Pacific Coast Conference, snaring Washington, California, UCLA, and USC.

Three Trojan booster and alumni organizations were found to have made under-the-table payments to athletes in excess of what the conference allowed for living expenses. According to newspaper reports, the most active of these groups, the Southern California Educational Foundation, revealed that it had paid $17,775 to 42 football players and two members of the track team. The Trojan Club allegedly paid $1,584 directly to three football players who were not eligible for grants-in-aid.

Meeting in San Francisco, PCC officials acted decisively by declaring 42 USC players ineligible for the 1956 sea-

The President's Council of the Pacific Coast Conference gathers for its 1957 meeting. The PCC slapped major sanctions on USC and three other West Coast schools the year before.

son, assessing fines, and banning the team from the Rose Bowl and other postseason appearances for two years. Washington received similar penalties, Cal slightly fewer, while UCLA was hit the hardest. It was banned from the postseason until 1960 and all its players ruled ineligible.

Administrators from the four universities argued for leniency. In early August, the PCC decided that while younger players would have to sit out an entire season, seniors could participate in five games of their choosing. The vote was 8–1, with Stanford insisting that the original ruling stand. "It was an endeavor to get nearer to justice in a situation where you cannot get perfect justice," Cal President Robert Gordon Sproul told reporters.

The Trojans fared surprisingly well that fall. After C. R. Roberts trampled Texas in the opener, the team finished with an 8–2 record that included victories over UCLA, Wisconsin, and Notre Dame, the final AP Poll placing them No. 18 in the nation. But the PCC sanctions were painful for a number of upperclassmen.

Roberts, a junior, had a breakout performance in 1956; he then had to sit out the next season. The penalties also hurt "Jaguar" Jon Arnett, one of USC's all-time greats. Arnett had been the team's leading rusher in 1954 and '55, winning All-America honors as a junior, and he figured to be in the thick of the Heisman Trophy race in 1956. He played marvelously through the first five games, rushing for 625 yards and scoring 6 touchdowns. But there would be no bronze trophy as the PCC forced him to sit out the final half of his senior season.

The Road Back

The USC football program was in turmoil. The team faced another year of sanctions from the PCC scandal, and its coach, Jess Hill, had moved upstairs to become athletic director. While news reports mentioned several potential candidates, including Bud Wilkinson of Oklahoma and Duffy Daugherty of Michigan State, the players circulated a petition in support of assistant coach Don Clark.

Clark had played left guard for the Trojans and was captain of the 1947 Rose Bowl team before joining the San Francisco 49ers in the NFL. He returned to the university in 1951 to work as an assistant under Hill. The players quickly took to him. In early February 1957, USC gave the 33-year-old a four-year contract.

It wasn't exactly a plum job. The Trojans had been sapped of veteran talent by the recruiting sanctions, so Clark needed to be creative. He dropped the multiple offense in favor of a "go, go, go" attack made popular at Oklahoma, where plays are run in quick succession to wear down the opposing defense. But the Trojans were facing a monstrous schedule that included four nationally ranked opponents. They lost the season opener to No. 13 Oregon State and slid downhill from there, finishing with a dismal 1–9 record.

After that, several things put them back on track. First, Clark was allowed to start recruiting in full again, and he signed the McKeever twins, Mike and Marlin, who would become All-Americans. He also simplified the offense, focusing on plays out of the T formation. USC responded with a 4–5–1 season in 1958, then improved to 8–2.

Despite the team's brightening prospects, Clark abruptly resigned after the 1959 season, saying: "I never intended to make coaching my career." No one knew it at the time, but he had altered the history of USC football a few months earlier by hiring a young assistant named John McKay.

Out with the Old

Two years passed and still resentments ran deep through the Pacific Coast Conference. The teams that had been sanctioned for improper payments to athletes harbored a grudge. Some schools complained about other schools lowering admission standards in an effort to sign more athletes. By the spring of 1958, the conference was falling apart. Attempts were made to patch old wounds, but when faculty representatives from the nine schools convened in the summer of 1959, the outcome was a foregone conclusion: By unanimous vote, they dissolved their 44-year-old union.

The funny thing is, a good chunk of the membership—USC, UCLA, Stanford, California, and Washington—immediately formed a new league, the Athletic Association of Western Universities. The arrangement seemed to work, and they eventually added former PCC schools Washington State, Oregon, and Oregon State. The foundation for the Pacific-10 Conference was in place.

The process of rebuilding a troubled football program began with the hiring of former guard Don Clark as head coach in 1957.

The Birth of a Legend

USC had gone almost three decades without a national title when a coach named John McKay arrived to lead the program back into the national spotlight.

No one knew what to make of John McKay. When USC introduced him as the new football coach in the winter of 1959, the media described him as "like-able" and "a devoted family man," grasping to describe the largely anonymous young assistant from Oregon who had

joined the Trojan staff less than a year earlier. Even McKay acknowledged: "I'm naturally surprised and, of course, thrilled with the opportunity. This happened so suddenly."

As it turned out, the team got a leader who could be alternately witty and standoffish, demanding and moody, a skilled tactician who could inspire without hollering. "Always the same demeanor," former tailback Anthony Davis recalled. "Every once in a while he would show a lot of emotion, but mostly he was a stern, General Patton-type." Above all, McKay was a winner, guiding the Trojans to nine bowl games and four national championships in 16 seasons. His undefeated 1972 team still ranks among the greatest in college football history.

"Coach McKay had such a tremendous presence," former UCLA coach Terry Donahue said. "There was an aura around him."

The son of a coal mine superintendent in West Virginia, McKay served as a tail gunner in World War II before returning home to play running back at Purdue and Oregon in the late 1940s. When his career ended by injury, he joined the Ducks' coaching staff and remained as an assistant for nine years before Don Clark lured him to Southern California.

His first two seasons as head coach were hardly auspicious, the team finishing with records of 4–6 and 4–5–1 as he tinkered with various offenses. In 1962, McKay settled on an early version of the I formation that he would make famous. USC went undefeated that season, hanging on for a 42–37 victory over Wisconsin in the Rose Bowl, winning the first of his national titles.

The players carry McKay off the field after a 25–0 victory over Notre Dame in 1962, his first of many wins over the Irish.

Over time, McKay refined his offense, nurturing the likes of Mike Garrett, O. J. Simpson, and Anthony Davis as "Tailback U" dared opposing defenses to stop them from pounding ahead with "Student Body Right" and "Student Body Left." The Trojans strung together one winning season after another as their coach continued to adapt.

After Notre Dame manhandled his team in 1966, McKay went looking for bigger linemen. When Oklahoma wreaked havoc with its wishbone offense, he added more speed to the roster. And while his offenses excelled, he quietly assembled tough defenses—the 1972 team was a culmination of this evolving philosophy, strong and fast, immensely talented on both sides of the ball.

Off the field, the coach's persona grew in a far different direction from the disciplinarian that players knew. Here was a man who could deliver one-liners on *The Tonight Show* with Johnny Carson and keep sportswriters laughing as he held court each night in a corner booth at Julie's, a restaurant near campus. He had become a prince of the city, and no one expected him to leave. But after the 1975 season, with repeated overtures from the NFL, the Tampa Bay Buccaneers lured him away.

His career in the pro ranks would be a roller-coaster ride. The Bucs suffered through a record 26-game losing streak, then reached the NFC championship in their fourth year, the quickest ascendance for an expansion team in league history. He remained with Tampa Bay for nine years before retiring, but that did not alter his legacy.

"Let me tell you who my dad is," J. K. McKay said years later at his father's memorial service. "He is the coach of the USC Trojans. That's what he always loved being."

Make 'em Laugh

Whether talking to reporters, sitting around Julie's restaurant with a few buddies, or sitting across from Johnny Carson on national television, John McKay kept his dry wit at the ready. A few memorable lines:

Asked why O. J. Simpson carried the ball so often: "Why not? It isn't very heavy. Besides, he doesn't belong to a union."

On the role of emotion in football: "It's overrated. My wife is emotional, but she's a lousy football player."

On intensity: "Intensity is a lot of guys who run fast."

When one of his players fielded the opening kickoff at Notre Dame, then promptly fell on his face: "My God, they shot him."

With his team losing 17–0 to the Irish in 1964, McKay told the players at halftime: "If you don't score more than 17 points, you'll lose." (They won 20–17.)

On recruiting his son, J. K. McKay: "I had a rather distinct advantage. I slept with his mother."

After a loss at Tampa Bay, McKay was asked about his team's execution: "I think it's a good idea."

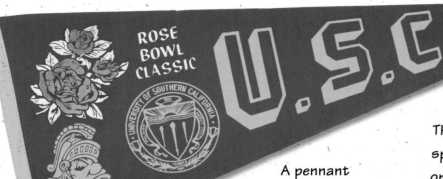

A pennant from the 1970 season. The Trojans defeated Alabama in the season opener but finished with a mediocre 6–4–1 record.

The media spotlight shone on running back O. J. Simpson during his two seasons at USC. He led the team to a national title in 1967 and won the Heisman Trophy the next year.

From Jerry Kramer's Best Selling Book: The Packers Down The Stretch

SPORT

DECEMBER 50c

O. J. Simpson: In Quest Of All The Prizes

The Day Denny McLain Won No. 30

O. J. SIMPSON, USC

The Uphill Struggle Of Arnold Palmer

USC vs UCLA

STAIRWAY 12 ROW 57 SEAT 16

FOOTBALL 1967 LOS ANGELES COLISEUM · SAT. NOV. 18/1:30 ESTABLISHED PRICE $6.00

John Morley TICKET MANAGER

DILLINGHAM TICKET CO., L.A.

For six dollars, fans got a seat at the 1967 game between USC and UCLA, which the Trojans won with a fourth quarter rally.

This football is signed by Mike Garrett, who won the 1965 Heisman Trophy and later became a very successful athletic director at USC.

The Tournament of Roses honored Hollywood in 1973, choosing "Movie Memories" as its theme. That year, the official game program for the Rose Bowl showed a film strip arching from the field where USC played Ohio State.

A thrilling win over Wisconsin in the Rose Bowl secured this 1962 national title trophy for the Trojans and their relatively new coach, John McKay.

USC did not choose cardinal and gold—as seen on this pin—as its official school colors until 1895.

Many Trojan fans wear all manner of team accessories, including tie clips, proclaiming their team loyalty.

The Horse. The Horse.

Former Notre Dame coach Ara Parseghian was once asked to describe his feelings about Traveler, USC's regal white horse. "Can you print it?" he replied. On a more serious note, Parseghian said: "It was one of those intimidating things. They'd come storming down there with that horse… it was right out of the Trojan days."

Traveler and his warrior rider are among the most recognized mascots in college sports. In addition to galloping across the Coliseum turf on Saturday afternoons, they have appeared in scores of Rose Parades, movies, and television commercials. Heisman Trophy–winning tailback Mike Garrett recalls the sensation of watching "the horse come prancing out onto the field, especially after we scored. Or if it was late in the game and we were driving, you would look over and see the horse, and it really inspired you. You got turned on."

A university administrator first spotted Richard Saukko leading a group of white horses in the Rose Parade on New Year's Day, 1961. The football team lacked a mascot—the mutt George Tirebiter had retired and a previous attempt to ride a rented horse in the Coliseum had failed. The school asked Saukko to give it a try, providing him with the leather vest and helmet that Charlton Heston wore in the film *Ben Hur.* That outfit proved too cumbersome, so Saukko kept the helmet but made his own leather costume, modeled after Tommy Trojan.

"As you come out into the crowd, it's just like riding into a blast furnace," he once said. "It's so hot and there's so much noise, you can't believe it. The players are yelling at me and giving me the victory sign."

The first Traveler was a brother to Silver of the TV show *Lone Ranger.* There have been others since—ranging in breed from Andalusian to Arabian to Tennessee Walker—but all have been pure white. According to folklore, O. J. Simpson decided to play for USC after seeing the horse on television. Former coach Ted Tollner said: "The number of athletes that we recruit who identify us with the Trojan horse is amazing. The kid could be from Iowa and the only time he's seen it is on television. They know the horse and the rider."

Tollner spoke of the power and mystique, adding: "It exemplifies the tradition of the football program at USC."

USC tried a number of mascots before settling on a white horse with armored rider in the early 1960s. Saukko and Traveler, who has become an icon of the game, are shown in 1972.

McKay Gets His First Title

John McKay said he was lucky to hang on as USC coach through his first two—decidedly mediocre—seasons. After his third year, there would be no more concerns about job security.

The 1962 Trojans represented a transition, a first step toward the classic McKay teams that followed. There was no dominating tailback. Instead, versatile Willie Brown led the team in rushing, interceptions, punt and kickoff returns, and was also second in receiving. Rotating quarterbacks Pete Beathard and Bill Nelsen combined for 18 touchdown passes against only three interceptions. The defense held opponents to one touchdown or less in eight games.

All of which was good enough for a national championship.

The season began with a 14–7 upset victory over eighth-ranked Duke, placing the unheralded Trojans in the Top 10. Each victory nudged them further up the polls and they sat at No. 1; then they defeated UCLA and Notre Dame by convincing scores in the final two weeks of the regular season. Only Wisconsin in the 1963 Rose Bowl stood between McKay and his first title.

Beathard dominated the action for most of the day in Pasadena, tossing four touchdown passes—two of them to star receiver Hal Bedsole—to give his team a 42–14 lead early in the fourth quarter. But just when it looked as if victory was certain, Wisconsin caught fire.

Quarterback Ron VanderKelen led the Badgers to three quick touchdowns, and special teams added a safety—a 23-point rally that closed the gap to 42–37. With the final seconds ticking away, USC recovered an onside kick and ran out the clock. It may not have been the most convincing way to secure a national championship, but as McKay told his players afterward, "Our intention was to win today... and what does the scoreboard say?"

The football team signed this ball commemorating their 1962 national championship.

Fullback Ben Wilson dives for a score against Wisconsin in the 1963 Rose Bowl. USC held on to win the game and a national title.

The Dawn of Tailback U

Before Mike Garrett became the first great USC tailback, he almost played for UCLA. Garrett wanted to enroll at the Westwood campus but, he recalls, the Bruin coaches "thought I was too small. They asked me to go to junior college." Coach John McKay offered him a scholarship at the last minute and soon realized the kid from East Los Angeles was something special.

The Trojans had just won the 1962 national championship with rotating quarterbacks Pete Beathard and Bill Nelsen, so the I formation was geared toward the pass. According to Garrett, when Beathard and Nelsen left for the NFL, McKay discovered that talented running backs were easier to find than quarterbacks. Chart the trajectory of Garrett's career from that point, and you can see the evolution of a USC tradition.

Tenacious and strong, he was perfectly suited for the new power offense. His carries and total yardage increased each season until, by 1965, the senior tailback had grown into a workhorse, rushing for a school record 1,440 yards and 13 touchdowns. He owned numerous NCAA and conference records and became only the second West Coast player to win the Heisman Trophy.

Hard-nosed Mike Garrett was a perfect fit for the power offense that John McKay wanted to play.

Ironically, the man who cast the mold for "Tailback U" never got a chance to play in the Rose Bowl. USC tied for the conference title in his junior season, but the membership voted for Oregon State to play on New Year's Day. The following year, the Trojans missed out on a trip to Pasadena when UCLA defeated them in the final minutes. Rarely emotional around players, McKay told his co-captain: "Sorry we didn't win that for you." But Garrett wasn't the type to brood, later telling the *Los Angeles Times*, "'SC is not designed to make you happy or make you perfect—it is designed to prepare you for reality." Besides, he wasn't done being a Trojan.

Almost 30 years later, after a career that spanned the NFL to law to business, Garrett returned to USC as athletic director. At a January 1993 news conference to announce his hiring, university President Steven B. Sample told the assembled crowd: "Mike Garrett not only knows the great Trojan athletic tradition, he helped create it." And in the winter of 2000 he would lift it to even greater heights, hiring a new football coach by the name of Pete Carroll.

Garrett became the first USC Trojan—and only the second player from the West Coast—to win the Heisman Trophy. His performance over three seasons set the standard for USC tailbacks to follow.

O. J. Leads the Way

With opening kickoff at Notre Dame Stadium only minutes away, John McKay ordered his players to stay put in the locker room. Two years earlier, in 1965, the Irish had kept USC waiting on the field in chilly weather and the Trojans had lost badly. This time, McKay wanted the home team out there first, even as an official threatened to call the game. "What does that mean?" McKay asked.

"It means Notre Dame wins 2–0 on a forfeit."

The coach replied, "That would be the best damn deal we've ever gotten in this stadium."

No one pushed the 1967 Trojans around, not with All-America tackle Ron Yary leading the way for the next great tailback, O. J. Simpson. Not with a dominating defense that featured lineman Tim Rossovich and linebacker Adrian Young. USC swept through its first four games, pushing aside the likes of Texas and Michigan State. On that day in South Bend—after both teams finally took the field—Simpson had a breakout performance with three touchdowns, as the defense grabbed seven interceptions in a 24–7 victory over the fifth-ranked Irish.

A few weeks later, the Trojans ran into an opponent they could not overwhelm: Mother Nature. On a rainy day in Corvallis, the game marred by a sloppy field, they lost in a 3–0 upset to Oregon State. But there was still time to rebound against top-ranked UCLA in the regular-season finale.

The crosstown rivalry featured a showdown between Simpson, on his way to an NCAA-best 1,543 yards, and

the Bruins' talented quarterback, Gary Beban. With USC trailing in the fourth quarter, the stage was set for one of the most memorable plays in college football history. Simpson took a seemingly ordinary handoff to the left, broke several tackles and bounced outside, then hesitated ever so slightly before shifting back across field and outracing the defense for a 64-yard touchdown that gave his team a 21–20 victory. "Well, gentlemen," McKay said afterward, "I guess I wasn't so stupid today."

Beban earned the Heisman Trophy that year, but Simpson got something even better. The Trojans were back on top of the polls, and this time they did not slip, handily defeating Indiana 14–3 in the Rose Bowl to earn the school's fifth national championship.

Simpson was so popular during his time at USC that he earned a personalized pennant.

O. J. Simpson dashes through the Notre Dame defense, leading top-ranked USC to one of the victories that added up to a national title in the 1967 season.

Crisp White Sweaters

Through the late 1960s, as the Trojans played in four consecutive Rose Bowls, the team drew crowds of 50,000 to 60,000 on most Saturday afternoons, with as many as 90,000 fans showing up for the rivalry games. They got something more for their money than just a football game.

Only male yell leaders had roamed the USC sidelines to that point, but with female cheerleaders becoming the norm, the university held tryouts in 1967. It was a somewhat controversial move on campus, and during those first few seasons, the USC song girls were considered upstarts, if not cheap imitations when compared to their more established counterparts at UCLA.

The USC squad was coached by Lindley Bothwell, a San Fernando Valley orange grower who had been a baseball player and yell leader at the university in the early 1920s. Within five years of that first game, Bothwell had guided his group to national prominence and a No. 1 ranking from the International Cheerleading Foundation. More importantly, the song girls became a part of Trojan football lore, every bit as essential as Traveler and the marching band. As for their trademark outfits, the crisp white sweaters and short skirts, Bothwell had a role in that, too.

The song girls (shown in 1978) became a part of USC folklore with the help of their first coach, Lindley Bothwell.

"The kids used to design their own uniforms—to get ten girls to agree on a pattern is terrible," he told the *Los Angeles Times* in 1980. "I chose the uniforms: All white, with a USC emblem on the sweater, cardinal and gold stripes on the skirt. The kids threw a fit, but now we have 50 high schools and colleges copying us."

There were other changes during the 1950s, '60s, and '70s. The team played before a national television audience for the first time in 1951, a loss to Notre Dame. As viewers got to know the Trojans, their stadium became more famous, too.

USC wasn't the only game at the Coliseum. UCLA and the Los Angeles Rams played there, and the NFL used it for the Pro Bowl as well as Super Bowls I and VII. The Dodgers squeezed in a diamond from 1958 to 1961. In 1967, Billy Graham drew 134,254 people to a religious gathering there.

A League of Their Own

If adversity begets strength, the Athletic Association of Western Universities was tough as nails by the 1960s. The league was created after scandals tore apart the Pacific Coast Conference. Comprised of USC, UCLA, California, Stanford, and Washington, the AAWU was known as the "Big Five"; it added Washington State to became the "Big Six."

The conference sent its champion to the Rose Bowl, and in 1946 (modified in 1960), they signed a deal to cement the annual match-up against a Big Ten opponent. But 1964 brought trouble. The AAWU presidents and chancellors met and admitted Oregon and Oregon State. Not everyone was thrilled.

By 1964, the AAWU had yet to devise a tiebreaking system. When USC and Oregon State tied for the title, the conference voted to determine the Rose Bowl representative. Despite the Trojans knocking off top-ranked Notre Dame, Oregon State won the vote.

In 1968, the new league formally adopted a new name: The Pacific-8 Conference.

The Juice

In 1968, the voters of the Downtown Athletic Club gave O. J. Simpson the Heisman Trophy by the largest margin in the history of the storied award.

It was the summer of 1966, and O. J. Simpson, a budding star at San Francisco City College, took a recruiting trip to Utah. The coach there, Mike Giddings, assigned a couple of players to show him around campus, saying: "If we get this guy, we're going to be good." One of the Utes who hosted Simpson on that visit? Offensive lineman and future USC offensive coordinator Norm Chow.

Simpson signed a letter of intent to play for the Utes, according to Giddings. But when he returned home to the Bay Area, tenacious USC assistant Marv Goux convinced him to stay in junior college for one more year, then attend USC the following year. As Chow explained years later, "the rest is history."

"The Juice" possessed all the prerequisites to become a great running back. Strength and speed. Dazzling moves. An uncanny knack for detecting the smallest cracks in the defense. With a big Trojan line leading the way, it did not take long for Simpson to burst onto the national scene, rushing for 1,543 yards as a junior. Fans across the nation saw him zigzag through the UCLA defense, scoring the game-winning touchdown that catapulted USC to a national championship.

"In a football game," he once said, "I just don't want to be touched."

The next fall, Simpson set an NCAA record by running for 1,709 yards during the regular season while leading his team to a second consecutive Rose Bowl. That put Simpson back on the All-America team and earned him the Heisman Trophy—USC's second in four years—by the biggest vote margin in history.

The records continued to fall in the professional ranks when the Buffalo Bills drafted Simpson with the No. 1 pick. In 1973, he became the first NFL player to run for more than 2,000 yards in a season. By the time of his retirement in 1979, he ranked second on the all-time rushing list.

Good looks and a confident smile carried him straight into a career after football, working as a television com-

Simpson runs in the second half of USC's loss to Ohio State in the 1969 Rose Bowl.

mentator and appearing in a commercial that showed him dashing through an airport, flashing some of his old moves. With roles in movies such as *The Naked Gun*, it appeared that nothing could stop him. Unfortunately, his peronal saga was far from over. But his later trials do not diminish his athletic achievements at USC and in the NFL, though they do tarnish his personal reputation.

Heart-stopping Finishes

It started with the first game of the season, the Trojans scoring two touchdowns in the last four minutes to defeat Minnesota. Then came fourth-quarter victories over Stanford and Washington and a touchdown with 1:12 remaining to win in rainy Oregon. Fans started calling the 1968 USC team by a new name: "The Cardiac Kids."

The Trojans had one more close call that year, scoring in the fourth quarter to tie Notre Dame, before losing to Ohio State in the Rose Bowl. O. J. Simpson collected his Heisman Trophy and went on to the pros. New offensive leaders replaced him—sophomore quarterback Jimmy Jones and tailback Clarence Davis—but the thrills weren't over.

In 1969, kicker Ron Ayala made a 34-yard field goal with no time remaining to defeat Stanford. After another tie at Notre Dame and a tight victory over California, Jones overcame a miserable start to throw a 32-yard touchdown pass with less than two minutes on the clock,

The USC Wild Bunch included (from left to right) Al Cowlings, Jimmy Gunn, Bubba Scott, Charles Weaver, and Tody Smith.

clinching a nail-biter against crosstown rival UCLA. This time, USC triumphed in Pasadena, pulling out a 10–3 victory against Michigan.

It wasn't just offense that kept the Trojans winning. The 1969 team featured the "Wild Bunch," perhaps the best defensive line in school history. Jimmy Gunn and Charles Weaver played on the ends with Al Cowlings and Tody Smith at tackle and Bubba Scott at middle guard. This unit tortured opposing quarterbacks on the way to producing no fewer than three All-Americans.

They got their nickname from a Sam Peckinpah film about an aging band of outlaws. After the USC linemen posed for a publicity shot dressed as gunslingers, fans screamed "Wild Bunch" whenever opponents threatened to score. "The objective of defense is to seek out the ball carrier and separate him from the ball," assistant coach Marv Goux explained. "Warner Brothers should consider our group for its next Western."

More Than a Game

All these years later, it is difficult to separate fact from fiction regarding the 1970 season opener at Alabama. This much is true: The Crimson Tide put an all-white team on the field in Birmingham that night. And USC fullback Sam "Bam" Cunningham—one of numerous black players in the Trojan lineup—powered his way to 135 yards and 2 touchdowns on just 12 carries.

But football was only part of the story in a game played against a backdrop of social conflict. Years after President Lyndon B. Johnson signed the Civil Rights Act of 1964, Alabama was just beginning to integrate its team. Some people claim that legendary coach Paul "Bear" Bryant scheduled the Trojans hoping to convince his team's boosters—and his state—that he should be allowed to recruit more African Americans.

When kickoff came around, there wasn't much drama on the field. Cunningham, a sophomore playing in his first college game, ran for two early scores and tailback Clarence Davis, a Birmingham native, added another receiving. The Alabama offense simply could not move the ball against USC's bigger, faster defense. By the fourth quarter, Coach John McKay pulled his starters as the Trojans cruised to a 42–21 victory. Legend has it that Bryant invited Cunningham back to the Crimson Tide locker room after the game and announced: "This is what a football player looks like." The publicity shy Cunningham has been quoted as saying he recalls talking to Bryant but does not remember that scene. Regardless, Alabama added more

This game ball from the USC–Alabama matchup is a treasured piece of USC history.

black players in the seasons to come, and an Alabama assistant coach, Jerry Claiborne, remarked, "Sam Cunningham did more to integrate Alabama in 60 minutes that night than Martin Luther King had accomplished in 20 years."

It was an otherwise forgettable season for the Trojans, who finished 6–4–1, but memories of the game live on. More than 30 years later, Cunningham returned to Alabama with friend and former teammate John Papadakis. As they dined at an upscale restaurant, all the black waiters and busboys stopped by to pay their respects said Papadakis, who coauthored a book about the game titled *Turning of the Tide*. Later, a cab driver asked if he could take them on a brief detour through his neighborhood. "There were all these people on the street," Papadakis said. "They just wanted to meet Sam."

USC fullback Sam Cunningham scored twice against Alabama in a 1970 game some believe helped integrate Southern football.

The showdown between UCLA quarterback Gary Beban and USC's O. J. Simpson in 1967 ranks as a highlight in the storied crosstown rivalry; it is also highlighted on this *Sports Illustrated* cover.

After a stellar career at USC in the early 1970s, Lynn Swann was inducted into the College Football Hall of Fame.

The Trojans' national title season in 1974 included a 15–15 tie against California.

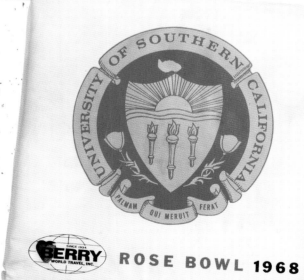

A seat cushion from the 1968 Rose Bowl, where USC defeated Indiana 14–3 to wrap up another national title.

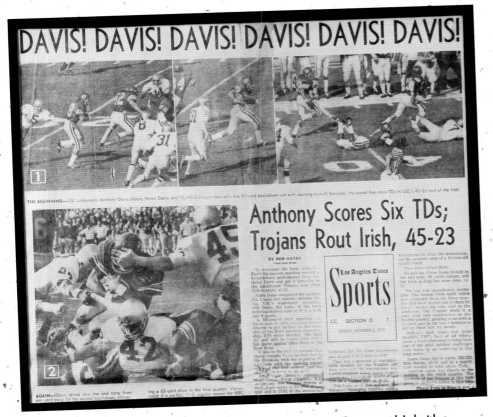

DAVIS! DAVIS! DAVIS! DAVIS! DAVIS! DAVIS!

Anthony Scores Six TDs; Trojans Rout Irish, 45-23

Anthony Davis had a knack for hurting Notre Dame, which the *Los Angeles Times* notes in its coverage of this stellar day against the Irish in 1972.

The Trojans eked out a 14–12 victory over UCLA to clinch the 1952 conference title. They later defeated Wisconsin in the Rose Bowl on New Year's Day.

TOURNAMENT OF ROSES

1969

USC vs OHIO STATE

TROJANS   BUCKEYES

The 1969 Rose Bowl was the first meeting of legendary coaches John McKay and Woody Hayes, and the game decided the national championship. Ohio State beat USC 27–16.

More Than Just Tailbacks

Not every great player who came through USC from 1951 through 1975 carried the football. "Tailback U" needed offensive linemen to lead the way and quarterbacks to keep opponents honest by passing. The team needed defense, too.

Start with the early 1950s and a halfback named Frank Gifford. His college career languished under coach Jeff Cravath, who relegated him to defense, kicking, and little else. Then Jess Hill took over in 1951 and turned the senior into an All-American. To appreciate what Gifford accomplished that season, consider his performance in USC's upset of top-ranked California. With the Trojans down by two touchdowns, he ran 69 yards for one touchdown, passed for another, and drove his team for the winning score.

The late 1950s brought the McKeever brothers, the first twins to be All-Americans. Mike played left guard and Marlin was a right end and fullback. Ron Mix joined the distinguished heritage of USC offensive linemen, a tradition that soon blossomed under John McKay and the power running of the I formation. Offensive tackle Ron

The little-used Frank Gifford blossomed in his senior year, taking over at halfback and becoming an All-American in 1951.

Yary became the first Trojan to win the Outland Trophy, awarded to the nation's best interior lineman. One after another, Marv Montgomery, John Vella, Steve Riley, and Bill Bain earned All-America honors for their ferocity in the trenches.

A unanimous All-American in 1972, tight end Charles Young helped the Trojans to a national title. Young was a first-round pick in the NFL draft, playing pro football for more than a decade and appearing in two Super Bowls.

Twin brothers Mike and Marlin McKeever were All-Americans in the late 1950s.

The passing game rose to prominence in the 1970s with two standout receivers. First came Charles "Tree" Young, deceptively quick for his size, a College Hall of Famer at tight end. Then Lynn Swann made consensus All-American in 1973, the start of a career that would see him become the most valuable player in Super Bowl X for the Pittsburgh Steelers. Neither big nor blazing fast, Swann made his mark as a smooth, seemingly effortless player. "A really bright guy," quarterback Mike Rae recalled. "He was able to get open and, of course, he had great hands."

McKay's never-ending search for strong, fast athletes carried over to the defensive side of the ball. It wasn't just the "Wild Bunch" on the line; his tenure also marked the beginning of a string of standout linebackers, starting with Damon Bame and Adrian Young, then Willie Hall and Richard "Batman" Wood, USC's first three-time first-team All-American. As a counterpart to the receivers, Artimus Parker and Charles Phillips made their marks in the defensive secondary.

Part of the Family

Pat Haden certainly wasn't the biggest quarterback, nor did he possess the strongest arm. It seems he excelled at only one thing: winning. In his three seasons on the field, he helped guide the Trojans to three Rose Bowls and two national championships.

But playing at USC meant more than football to him. An excellent student and future Rhodes Scholar, Haden grew up as best friends with the coach's son, J. K., and he lived with the McKays when his own parents moved away before his senior year in high school. He and J. K. then became a potent quarterback-receiver combination in college.

Years later, they still sound like brothers. Asked if opposing defenses feared J. K., Haden said: "I'm not sure they even guarded him." To which J. K. responded: "As you might know, Pat is so short that I could not make eye contact with him. I couldn't even make forehead contact."

Lynn Swann starred in the 1970s.

The Best Ever

Astute recruiting. A knack for adapting to the changes in college football. An ironclad determination to win. All of John McKay's best qualities over a celebrated career came to a head in 1972 with his greatest team yet.

That year, USC possessed the quintessential I formation offense built around a strong and fast line, a powerful lead blocker in fullback Sam "Bam" Cunningham, and a young Anthony Davis at tailback. Mike Rae and Pat Haden shared quarterback duties, throwing to future College and Pro Football halls of fame receiver Lynn Swann. Just as important, the

With tailback Anthony Davis in the backfield—and a defense that shut down opponents—the Trojans assembled their most powerful team to date in 1972.

coaches had assembled a defense featuring All-America linebacker Richard Wood and a lock-down secondary.

"USC's not the number one team in the country," Washington State coach Jim Sweeney quipped. "The Miami Dolphins are better."

The season started with a trip to Arkansas, where the Trojans dismantled the fourth-ranked Razorbacks 31–10, a victory that lifted them to No. 1 in the polls. There was

nothing fancy about the schemes or play calling as they won the next three games by a combined score of 157–32. "We had so much talent," Rae said. "We were just a power team, and we ran right at people."

Around mid-season, Rae realized the '72 team was bound for greatness. The Trojans were playing on a rain-soaked field at Oregon and had scored the game's first touchdown, but the quarterback/kicker missed the extra-point attempt. On the sidelines, McKay was furious. "It was just one point, but he was really upset," Rae said. Despite the sloppy conditions, USC prevailed 18–0 that afternoon. It became apparent the coach would not let his players falter or stumble.

No opponent came closer than nine points that season as Davis took care of tenth-ranked Notre Dame almost single-handedly, scoring six touchdowns—two of them on kickoff returns—to fuel a 45–23 victory. Everyone had a big day at the Rose Bowl. Cunningham leaped over the pile at the line of scrimmage, landing in the end zone no fewer than four times. Rae had an efficient performance. Davis ran for 157 yards. USC trampled Ohio State 42–17, not only winning the national championship but also becoming the first team in history to receive every first-place vote in both the AP and UPI polls.

Sam Cunningham helped USC finish a perfect season by scoring four touchdowns in a 42–17 win over Ohio State in the 1973 Rose Bowl.

1974: A Season to Remember

J. K. McKay, the coach's son, grabs a fourth-quarter scoring pass from Pat Haden to help the Trojans to an 18–17 win over Ohio State in the 1975 Rose Bowl and a share of the national title.

People might forget that the 1974 season started badly for the Trojans. Ranked among the top teams in the nation, they lost the opener at Arkansas and struggled occasionally in the weeks that followed, suffering a tie against California. But viewed through the prism of time, that year was all about two games.

"The Comeback" against Notre Dame ranks among the greatest victories in Trojan football history. It wasn't just Anthony Davis returning the second-half kickoff for a touchdown—there were so many big plays. Receiver J. K. McKay recalled an impromptu connection with quarterback Pat Haden after USC had charged back from a 24–6 deficit. "I was supposed to run a curl, but Notre Dame had blown the coverage so I ran to the post and looked back hoping that Pat would see me," he said. "I recall hearing the crowd roar. Then all of a sudden here came the ball, looking like Pat was throwing a grenade out of a foxhole." The pass went for a touchdown, and the Trojans were on their way to a 55–24 victory.

The Rose Bowl was every bit as exciting. Third-ranked Ohio State led by a touchdown in the final minutes when Haden threw deep again, hitting McKay in the far corner of the end zone. With USC trailing by one, coach John McKay called for a two-point attempt. His players weren't surprised because he had gambled in big games before. This time, Haden rolled out to his right and looked for J. K., who was covered, then spotted Shelton Diggs along the back line. The pass was low but precise, with Diggs falling to the turf to make the catch.

The Trojans had an 18–17 victory and, when Alabama lost to Notre Dame in the Orange Bowl that night, they also had a national championship.

The Trojans faced Ohio State's fierce ground game on New Year's Day.

Changing Times

1976–1997

The winning continues under a new coach, John Robinson, but when he unexpectedly walks away from the game, the Trojans fall into a decline. No more national championships, no more Heisman trophies. Through the 1980s and '90s, a once-mighty program struggles to recapture its glory.

Larry Smith (right) led USC to three straight Rose Bowls in the late 1980s, but he was fired soon after. He poses with Michigan's Bo Schembechler before the 1989 game.

At the 65th Rose Bowl Game (see ticket above), in 1979, USC beat Michigan 17–10. In the era described in this chapter, USC and Michigan played each other four times; USC won three of those contests.

Michael Harper scores a controversial touchdown—in this photo he appears to fumble short of the goal line—as the Trojans defeat Notre Dame in 1982.

Following a Legend

Trojan fans might not have known much about John Robinson when he took over at USC in 1976, but they soon found themselves cheering for "The Fat Man." Over the course of two stints at the school, through 1997, Robinson carved out a spot among the winningest coaches in Trojan history with a record of 104–35–4. He led USC to eight postseason games, including four Rose Bowls, and a national title in 1978.

For the first time in more than 16 years, USC needed a football coach. John McKay went to the NFL, and the Trojans had some very big shoes to fill. They turned to a former assistant who, much like McKay had been, was virtually unknown to fans. John Robinson had played under McKay at Oregon in the late 1950s and remained there as an assistant for a dozen years before joining the Trojan staff as offensive coordinator in the early 1970s. He left for one season to coach with the Oakland Raiders. That's when USC came calling.

Robinson was the perfect man for the job. He knew enough about the program to continue the traditions that McKay had established, a team based on power running and strong defense. At the same time, he set about modernizing the I formation. "The tailback was still the star," Robinson explained. "But the game was evolving, and we felt like we needed to expand the passing game. And we put more emphasis on the receivers, too."

Helping in this effort was a staff that blended longtime assistant Marv Goux with an impressive array of newcomers, including future NFL coach Norv Turner, future UCLA coach Bob Toledo, and a young offensive wizard named Paul Hackett, who would one day take over at USC. While it would be wrong to call the transition seamless—the Trojans were stunned by Missouri in their first game under the new guy—the team rebounded impressively, winning four bowl games and a national championship in Robinson's first four seasons. "He was a players' coach," quarterback Paul McDonald recalled. "Not a guy to yell and scream. Very encouraging."

The string of great USC tailbacks continued with Ricky Bell, Charles White, and Marcus Allen. At quarterback, an erratic Vince Evans matured into a winner and was followed by McDonald, among the best ever to play the posi-

Mr. Trojan

For all the big names that came and went, all the players and coaches, one man stuck with USC football across four decades. In many ways, the gruff-talking Marv Goux was the heart and soul of the program.

"Mr. Trojan" started as an undersize linebacker in the early 1950s, playing through the pain of a back injury that left him hunched over "like I was looking for nickels," he once joked. An assistant under three coaches, including John McKay and John Robinson, Goux was known for his fiery personality and his devotion to the team. Even when he was implicated in a scandal near the end of his career—he was caught scalping tickets and funneling cash to players in 1982— Goux insisted he was acting out of loyalty.

Long after he retired, USC frequently called him back to speak before big games. "Marv definitely was the anchor of the team," tailback Anthony Davis said. "You had to respect him."

Marv Goux was a tough, beloved assistant.

tion at USC. The defense was led by All-Americans that included linebacker Dennis Johnson, safety Ronnie Lott, and nose guard George Achica.

But the good times would not last forever. The Trojans began to falter in the early 1980s, and Robinson's career took off on a roller-coaster ride. In 1982, he announced his coaching days were over. After a short period as a university administrator, he became head coach of the Los Angeles Rams, where he turned Eric Dickerson into a record-setting running back. That job lasted until his firing in 1991, at which point—another surprise—USC brought him back.

"John Robinson II" had its high points, as the team worked its way back toward prominence with victories in the Cotton and Rose bowls. But the Trojans struggled against rivals Notre Dame and UCLA, and talk of national championships soon gave way to grumbling that Robinson wasn't as driven as he had been the first time around.

After the Trojans suffered mediocre seasons in 1996 and '97, the athletic director—former Heisman Trophy winner Mike Garrett—made a change. The move turned into a PR nightmare, with dueling news conferences and Robinson claiming that Garrett had fired him on his answering machine. Yet, as messy as this ending was, it could not diminish the legacy of a coach who followed a legend and found a way to become a winner in his own right.

John Robinson managed one of the toughest tricks in sports— following in the footsteps of a legend. He poses beside a portrait of the renowned John McKay.

Bouncing Back

Everyone knows the Trojans got off to a rocky start in 1976, losing their opener by three touchdowns to underdog Missouri. But the record books don't show another blunder that John Robinson suffered in his first

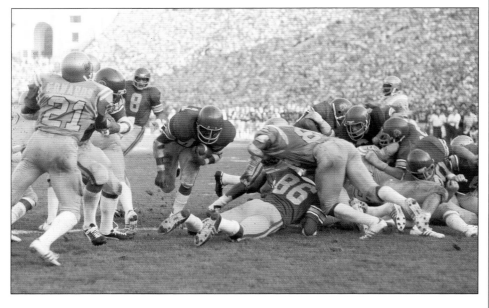

Tailback Ricky Bell had the moves to avoid tacklers, but he preferred to plow straight ahead. Here, he busts through the UCLA defense.

season, one that occurred a few months later. Leading his team out of the Coliseum tunnel for the UCLA game, he tripped and was overrun by players charging onto the field, the whole thing caught on national television. The next day, he got a call from close friend and Oakland Raiders coach John Madden. "I saw you on TV," Madden said. "You fell down. Boy, did you go down hard."

An upset loss and a stumble. Those were perhaps the only mistakes in an otherwise brilliant season.

That year, USC relied primarily on Ricky Bell, who at 6'2" and 218 pounds was a bigger, stronger version of the prototypical I formation tailback. "He could make you miss, but he didn't bother," Robinson said. "Ricky tried to run over you." And when opposing defenses crowded the line of scrimmage to contain him, the passing game kicked into gear. Quarterback Vince Evans, who had completed only 31.3 percent of his throws the previous season, quickly matured under Robinson's tutelage to become a solid contributor.

Stung by the Missouri loss, the players took out their frustration on Oregon the following week, 53–0, then rolled over Big Ten opponents Purdue and Iowa. They continued to build momentum through the conference schedule and into November, spoiling UCLA's undefeated record with a 24–14 upset win at the Coliseum. After edging past Notre Dame in the regular-season finale, they were headed for the Rose Bowl to face a Michigan team that led the nation in rushing, scoring, and total offense.

New Year's Day did not start well, not with Bell knocked unconscious in the first series, but USC was accustomed to dealing with early setbacks. Freshman tailback Charles White stepped into the lineup, giving fans a glimpse of the future as he rushed for 114 yards and a touchdown. Evans added another score, and the defense stopped Michigan cold for a 14–6 victory. Robinson, despite losing the opener and falling flat on his face, became only the second coach in Pac-10 history to win the Rose Bowl in his debut season.

White's performance in the 1977 Rose Bowl was just a glimpse of his future. It included the Heisman, which he noted when he signed this football.

"A Chemistry Thing"

No one knew quite what to expect in the fall of 1978. The Trojans still had Charles White at tailback, but could they improve on the 8–4 record of the year before? Could junior Paul McDonald fill the starting role at quarterback? Preseason polls offered some hope, placing USC in the Top 10. The third game of the season the team began to catch fire.

A bruising victory over top-ranked Alabama launched USC into the national championship hunt. White was on his way to 1,859 yards and got help from McDonald, an accurate passer who had time to throw behind guards Pat Howell and Brad Budde. The defense, led by future Hall of Fame safety Ronnie Lott, limited opponents to less than a dozen points a game. But talent was only part of the equation. "It was a chemistry thing," McDonald explained. "We had good people on that team." After a loss to Arizona State, the Trojans bounced back with five straight victories.

"We just kind of came together," coach John Robinson said. "I think Paul McDonald was a big reason for that."

Southern Discomfort

Birmingham was still hot and muggy in late September. USC had traveled east to face Alabama and, after warm-ups, the players returned to their locker room feeling worn out. Many of them sprawled across the cement floor, hoping to cool down. "I remember thinking, 'This isn't good,'" quarterback Paul McDonald said. "The humidity zaps you."

But when kickoff came around, with a crowd of 77,313 buzzing at Legion Field, the Trojans caught their second wind. The offensive line dominated a brutally physical game, with Charles White rushing for 199 yards. "I don't remember ever playing against a tailback who can run like White," Alabama coach Paul "Bear" Bryant said. The defense was just as strong, shutting down the top-ranked Crimson Tide, as seventh-ranked USC scored a 24–14 upset victory.

November brought a showdown against Notre Dame. With USC leading 24–6, the Irish threatened their version of "The Comeback," scoring three touchdowns in the fourth quarter. They took a 1-point lead with 46 seconds remaining, but it wasn't enough. McDonald hurried his offense down field, leaving kicker Frank Jordan two seconds to make a 37-yard field goal for the win.

That season, the Rose Bowl matched third-ranked USC against fifth-ranked Michigan in a low-scoring battle. McDonald passed for one touchdown, White dove three yards for another—it was a controversial score—and the defense took over, preserving a 17–10 Trojan win. Now poll voters had to decide. The Associated Press awarded its national title to Alabama, even though USC had defeated the Crimson Tide in Birmingham only a few months earlier. The Trojans took the top spot in the UPI poll.

The 1978 team was known for offensive stars such as tailback Charles White and quarterback Paul McDonald. But future Hall of Fame safety Ronnie Lott (right) led a strong defense.

Physical, Nasty, Aggressive

Blood flowed from his lacerated nose. His body felt weak from the flu. But with time running out in the 1980 Rose Bowl, his team behind by six points, Charles White wanted the football. Coach John Robinson couldn't say no, and White responded by ramming into the Ohio State defense again and again. Six times he ran, gaining 71 yards on the drive; he capped that mammoth effort by plunging across the goal line to give USC a 17–16 victory over Ohio State.

"He could go and go and go," said Paul McDonald, his quarterback that season. "Take a shot, get hammered, and come back for more."

USC tailbacks had to be tough in those days, carrying the ball 30 to 40 times a game. "We always believed that we were going to wear the other guy down," Robinson said. "Charlie fit the category of what you wanted. He wasn't big, nor was he extremely fast, but he was a physical, nasty, aggressive runner." And White could do more than run.

Earlier that season, against Notre Dame, he was called upon to block a larger defender. "You don't know this about him. He was an explosive blocker," McDonald said. "He leveled the guy, who was like 230 pounds. Just flattened him."

White had been a star at nearby San Fernando High School, before becoming a precocious freshman who burst onto the scene by replacing an injured Ricky Bell in the 1977 Rose Bowl. Consider a partial list of his top performances in the years that followed: 261 yards against Notre Dame, 247 against Ohio State in the 1980 Rose Bowl, 243 against Washington, and 221 against Stanford. As a senior, he averaged a whopping 186 yards a game to finish his college career as the second leading rusher in NCAA history with a total of 5,598 regular-season yards.

The Trojans rode his brand of determination to four consecutive bowl victories: three in the Rose, one in the Bluebonnet. White left as a two-time All-American and, finally, USC's third Heisman Trophy winner. He shrugged it all off, telling reporters after his Rose Bowl–winning touchdown: "That's our style, our game."

Eleven years after O. J. Simpson, tailback Charles White became USC's third Heisman Trophy winner in 1979.

White rushed for more than 100 yards in 31 of the 48 games he played for USC. In 1996, he became a member of the College Football Hall of Fame.

A Place in History

The unbeaten streak began after that midseason loss to Arizona State in 1978. The surprising Trojans finished with eight straight victories and a national championship; they returned the next fall as favorites to repeat. They hit a bump in the road against Stanford, taking a 21–0 halftime lead before crawling into a shell offensively, allowing the Cardinals to score three second-half touchdowns. A 21–21 tie cost them a second title but kept the run going.

Players from that era insist they did not spend much time thinking about the record book or all of those victories piling up. They simply expected to win, and this expectation fostered a confidence that helped them prevail regardless of the circumstances. Along with lopsided scores, there were narrow escapes against Washington and Louisiana State, and Ohio State in the Rose Bowl.

Even after they were caught up in a scandal at the beginning of the 1980 season—investigators discovered that USC and four other Pac-10 schools had falsified transcripts and fabricated credits for players—USC refused to waver. So the end came as a shock.

It came on November 15 in a 20–10 loss to Washington at the Coliseum. The Trojans outgained the Huskies by almost two to one, with tailback Marcus Allen rushing for 216 yards, but that wasn't enough to outweigh eight turnovers, poor special teams play, and the loss of quarterback Gordon Adams, who left with a knee injury. No one cared that they had established a 28-game mark, a school record that would stand for more than two decades. John Robinson summed up the mood when he said: "It was a day of extreme frustration for us."

5 45 101
TUNNEL ROW SEAT
ENTER GATE C

1980 PASADENA ROSE BOWL GRANDDADDY OF THEM ALL in Intercollegiate Football
Tuesday, January 1, 1980 2 p.m.
Established Price $18.00
Admission Tax   .50
Total: $18.50
Free Automobile Parking

Pete Carroll's first Rose Bowl appearance was in 1980 (see ticket above), as a secondary coach for Ohio State.

Missing the Point

Most people, when they think back on the 1980 Rose Bowl, recall Charles White carrying his team to victory with a fourth-quarter touchdown run. Coach John Robinson has a slightly different memory. In the waning seconds, the Trojans had possession of the ball near the Ohio State goal line. They were leading, so Robinson instructed his quarterback to take a knee.

A couple friends gave him odd looks afterward, but the coach thought nothing of it, leaving the next day for the Hula Bowl All-Star Game in Hawaii. Not until returning to Los Angeles did he realize the Trojans had been six-point favorites and that by running out the clock, they had disappointed countless gamblers by failing to cover the spread. "When I came back, I must have had 200 letters on my desk. They all began with the same salutation: 'You son of a [bleep]. . . .'"

The crowd celebrates USC's 1980 Rose Bowl win.

Marcus Allen Answers the Call

Nothing in Marcus Allen's résumé suggested that he would someday rank among the best tailbacks in USC history. As a high school star in San Diego, he played quarterback and defensive back, and the Trojans recruited him to bolster their secondary. But it did not take long for coaches to see that he should be carrying the football. There was only one problem—he had to wait for two years behind Charles White.

That meant standing on the sideline in 1978, appearing briefly in a handful of games. The

Tailback Marcus Allen, a Heisman Trophy receiver, was a versatile athlete who led USC in receptions his last two seasons.

following season, Robinson decided the sophomore "was too good not to play," so the Trojans converted him into an undersized fullback. This new role gave Allen a chance to display his athleticism by catching passes out of the backfield but also forced him to block much larger opponents. And when he finally got a chance to start at tailback in 1980, things didn't go easily.

Allen had never been an every-down runner. Mike Garrett offered him hints on how to attack the hole, and some called for Robinson to switch him back to fullback. "I didn't realize how much pressure there is to the position," Allen told the *Los Angeles Times*. His breakthrough came in late September when he rushed for 216 yards

and 2 TDs in a victory over Minnesota. From there, his confidence grew and he developed a knack for slicing through gaps in the line. His 1,563 yards that season foreshadowed bigger things.

The fall of 1981 began with 210 yards and 4 touchdowns against Tennessee, prompting the Volunteers coach Johnny Majors to remark: "He picks his holes as well as any back I've seen in my coaching career." The yardage accumulated as Allen led USC to victories over Indiana and second-ranked Oklahoma. Criticism was replaced with talk of a historic season.

Allen made good on all of the speculation, breaking a slew of NCAA records as he rushed for 212 yards a game to finish with an unprecedented 2,342 yards during the regular season. The Trojans faltered at the end of the season, but Allen cemented his legacy by capturing the Heisman Trophy.

A Marcus Allen signed football is a cherished piece of memorabilia for a USC fan.

A Pro's Pro

The play began with Marcus Allen running left, looking for a hole that would not open. Reversing direction, he almost got caught in the backfield but he slipped away and cut upfield. Then he turned on the jets. Seventy-four yards and several missed tackles later, the Los Angeles Raiders running back had sprinted for a record-setting touchdown against the Washington Redskins in Super Bowl XVIII.

That run served as a signature moment for Allen's professional career with the Raiders and later the Kansas City Chiefs. Over the course of 16 seasons, he was a Rookie of the Year, six-time Pro Bowler, and MVP of both the regular season and that Super Bowl. By the time of his Hall of Fame induction, Allen was considered one of the best short-yardage runners ever. He also stood as the first player in NFL history with more than 10,000 yards rushing and 5,000 yards receiving.

A Timeout and a Laugh

The game of the year—No. 1 USC versus No. 2 Oklahoma—had come down to the final seconds with the Trojans needing a touchdown to win. They had driven deep into Sooner territory when coach John Robinson called a timeout and summoned his young quarterback, John Mazur, to the sideline. "He was a sophomore, and he was scared to death," Robinson recalled. "His eyes were flashing back and forth." The coach was feeling a bit nervous himself, but this was no time to panic. He told Mazur to forget about the packed Coliseum and the national television audience.

"I said, 'Hey, this is a big picnic. Nobody cares who wins,'" Robinson recalled. "He looked at me like I was crazy, and we both started laughing."

> **"He [Mazur] was a sophomore, and he was scared to death."**
>
> **Coach John Robinson**

For much of that September afternoon in 1981, Oklahoma had threatened to run away with the game, as a trio of dangerous backs—Stanley Wilson, Buster Rhymes, and Chet Winters—gained big chunks of yardage in the wishbone offense. But the wishbone was prone to turnovers, and the Sooners fumbled ten times, losing five to USC, allowing the Trojans to close the gap to 24–21 with less than five minutes remaining.

Marcus Allen, who rushed for 208 yards that day, sparked USC's final drive with a pair of runs, and Mazur completed two clutch passes. On second-and-goal at the 7-yard line, the quarterback threw to Allen in the end zone, but tight end Fred Cornwell mistakenly jumped for the ball and tipped it away. Then came the last-second timeout and a laugh with Robinson. The Trojans called pretty much the same play on third down, and with Allen covered, a scrambling Mazur looked to Cornwell. The young tight end made up for his earlier gaffe, catching the pass for a touchdown and a memorable 28–24 victory.

A packed Coliseum crowd erupts as little-known USC tight end Fred Cornwell catches a last-second pass from John Mazur to help the No. 1 Trojans defeat No. 2 Oklahoma in the much-hyped 1981 game.

"He Tried His Best"

Following the highly successful John Robinson, Ted Tollner went 26–20–1 over four seasons, a winning record but not good enough for USC fans accustomed to national titles.

The week before the Notre Dame game in 1982, word leaked out that John Robinson was resigning as coach. The fans adopted a rallying cry, "Win One for the Fat Man," and the Trojans responded with a 17–13 comeback victory. Tailback Michael Harper scored a controversial touchdown—he might have fumbled shy of the goal line—with 48 seconds remaining. After the cheering subsided, the team had itself a new leader.

The bespectacled Ted Tollner was known as a passing guru, working with quarterbacks at San Diego State and Brigham Young before joining the USC staff in 1982 as Robinson's offensive coordinator. That November, he was hurriedly promoted to the head coach's job. "This is obviously a big day in my life," he told reporters. "To be a part of USC is all a man in my profession could ever ask for."

The Trojans were in the midst of another round of NCAA sanctions, banned from the postseason after an investigation found them guilty of recruiting violations and funneling cash from ticket sales to the players. The team finished 4–6–1 in Tollner's first season, their first losing record since 1961. Things improved somewhat thereafter—USC reached the Rose Bowl in 1984, defeating Ohio State—but after two wildly successful decades, the program slowly faded from the national spotlight.

Instead of playing in Pasadena each New Year's Day, USC found itself invited to second-tier bowl games. Even worse, Tollner went 1–7 against traditional rivals UCLA and Notre Dame, his tenure marking the start of a 13-year winless streak to the Irish. It was an untenable situation in the eyes of boosters spoiled by halcyon days gone by. Though players described Tollner as knowledgeable and fair, the type of coach who hardly ever yelled, his days were clearly numbered.

Athletic director Mike McGee announced Tollner's firing shortly before the end of the 1986 season, making him the first USC coach to be dismissed since Jeff Cravath in 1950. The team subsequently lost to Auburn in the Citrus Bowl, sending him off with a 26–20–1 record over four years.

"I thought he was a good man and he tried his best," said Sam Anno, a linebacker who later coached at USC. "It was a tough situation."

Football in the Far East

It was an up-and-down season for the Trojans. In the fall of 1985, they slipped to 4–5 before rebounding for an upset victory over eighth-ranked UCLA, freshman quarterback Rodney Peete sneaking across the goal line with 1:13 remaining on the clock. Then came a different kind of regular-season finale as the team flew to Tokyo to play Oregon in a game dubbed "The Mirage Bowl."

Jet-lagged players found themselves assigned to tiny rooms with the beds pushed together. The people were friendly but not entirely familiar with American football. At Tokyo Olympic Memorial Stadium, where USC won an uneventful game by the score of 20–6, organizers festooned half the crowd in cardinal and gold, the other half in Oregon green and yellow. "There was a sign or a signal when to cheer but it got screwed up and they started cheering all the time," linebacker Sam Anno said. "It was crazy."

Doing It the Hard Way

The first time Keith Byars touched the ball in the 1985 Rose Bowl, the Ohio State running back busted loose for 50 yards. The leading rusher in college football that season, Byars figured to have a big day against the Trojans, who finally shoved him out of bounds at the 5-yard line. The USC defensive players recall looking at each other and thinking: "Oh no."

That season had started well enough. USC rebounded from an early loss to Louisiana State to win six in a row, including an upset victory over top-ranked Washington at the Coliseum. The win assured a trip to the Rose Bowl for second-year coach Ted Tollner and gave fans renewed hope. But then came losses to UCLA and Notre Dame—turnover-filled games that weren't even close—so 18th-ranked USC headed for Pasadena as an underdog to sixth-ranked Ohio State.

The Trojans were led by an emotional reserve quarterback, Tim Green, who had replaced injured starter Sean

Feisty reserve quarterback Tim Green celebrates after guiding underdog USC to a winning season and a 20–17 upset victory over Ohio State in the 1985 Rose Bowl.

Salisbury. Green had talented receivers and a 1,000-yard tailback in Fred Crutcher, but the team's real strength was a defensive unit featuring All-America linebackers Jack Del Rio and Duane Bickett. "That season was about the seniors," receiver Lonnie White said. "The players had some heart."

After Byars's big gain, the defense made Ohio State settle for three points and put a lid on the dangerous back the rest of the way. Green threw two touchdown passes, kicker Steve Jordan added two 51-yard field goals, and though the Buckeyes made a late run, USC held on for a 20–17 victory. "Football is not a game of stats. It's physical, with power and hitting," Tollner told the *Los Angeles Times.* "We're not a pretty team but we did it the hard way, just as we have all season."

On a team led by defensive stars such as linebackers Jack Del Rio and Duane Bickett, tailback Fred Crutcher provided much of the offense for the 1984 team. Crutcher rushed for 1,155 yards.

An Outsider Takes Over

Larry Smith and his quarterback, Rodney Peete, watch an extra-point attempt in 1988's big win over UCLA. Smith's tough-minded approach to coaching, which had transformed losing programs at Tulane and Arizona into winners, translated into a 44–25–3 record and five bowl appearances over his six seasons at the helm of the Trojans.

The Trojans had slipped into mediocrity and, with Ted Tollner fired as coach, needed someone to rebuild the program. For the first time since Howard Jones, they turned to a man with no connection to the university.

Larry Smith grew up playing football in Ohio and got his start coaching high school in the town of Lima. The famed Bo Schembechler hired him as an assistant at Miami of Ohio in 1967, brought him along to Michigan two years later, and his career took off from there. By 1987, he had earned a national reputation for transforming Tulane and Arizona. His next project would be the Trojans. "He was a good man and a good football coach," athletic director Mike Garrett recalled. "When he came to USC, he brought a tough-minded approach and solid fundamentals, and he produced some very successful teams here."

USC made it to the Rose Bowl in each of his first three seasons and came within one loss of contending for a national championship in 1988. Over the course of six years, he amassed a 44–25–3 record, missing the postseason only once. "When Larry Smith came in, there were a lot of good players but the missing ingredients were organiza-

tion and discipline," receiver John Jackson said. "Discipline was his mantra. Nobody questioned it."

The Trojans of that era featured NFL-caliber talent on offense with quarterback Rodney Peete, lineman Tony Boselli, and receiver Curtis Conway. The defenses were led by All-Americans such as linebacker Junior Seau and safety Mark Carrier. But Smith had a different concept of the tailback—smaller and quicker, with fewer carries—and not everything went smoothly during his tenure.

Too many seasons ended badly, with slip-ups against Notre Dame and UCLA and losses in four of those five bowl games. Smith was not as personable as John McKay or John Robinson, and fans began to question his recruiting. Ultimately, the same tough-mindedness that helped him reshape the program might have been his undoing as he struggled to manage a gifted but capricious quarterback named Todd Marinovich. Television cameras caught them arguing on the sideline during a loss to Michigan State at the 1990 John Hancock Bowl. USC stumbled to subpar records the next two seasons, and after another lackluster bowl performance—an upset loss to Fresno State in the 1992 Freedom Bowl—Smith was fired.

1988: The Year That Almost Was

The fall of 1988 marked an anniversary for USC football—a century had gone by since that first ragtag group of players assembled on campus—but there were other reasons to celebrate. A decade removed from their last national championship, the Trojans had the look of a team that was back on top.

The season began with a convincing win at Boston College and, a few weeks later, a victory over third-ranked Oklahoma. One by one, Pacific-10 opponents fell by the wayside as senior quarterback Rodney Peete revved up the offense. The defense was equally impressive with Mark Carrier and Cleveland Colter anchoring the secondary. It seemed like the only thing that could stop USC was the measles; Peete fell ill before the UCLA game. He was hospitalized for several days amid much concern, and players from both teams were immunized and officials wondered if the game should be postponed.

The senior climbed out of bed just in time to lead his team to a 31–22 win over the Bruins and their talented quarterback, Troy Aikman. The win clinched a trip to Pasadena and set up an even bigger match-up the following week: No. 1 Notre Dame versus No. 2 USC.

Again, there was pregame drama as Peete got laryngitis and Notre Dame suspended two of its best players for showing up late to team functions. But once the game

Quarterback Rodney Peete eludes a Notre Dame pass rusher but could not lead the No. 2 Trojans past the No. 1 Irish in a crucial game at the end of the 1988 regular season.

began, the outcome was never in doubt. USC made all the mistakes while the Irish made all the big plays. It started with quarterback Tony Rice completing a 55-yard bomb from his own end zone, which softened the defense for a 65-yard touchdown run soon after. Cornerback Stan Smagala returned an interception 64 yards for another score. USC came away from the 27–10 loss a disheartened team.

In the Rose Bowl, the Trojans opened a 14–3 lead against underdog Michigan but faltered in the second half. The defense could not stop the run, and the offense kept misfiring with penalties and turnovers as Michigan scored twice in the fourth quarter to win 22–14. A year of celebration had ended on a down note. "I truly think we didn't play with the same fire and emotion," receiver John Jackson said. "The same spark wasn't there."

Peete dives over the goal line for one of his two touchdowns in the first half of the 1989 Rose Bowl against Michigan. In a season that fell just short of expectations, USC could not hold onto its lead, losing 22–14.

CHARLES WHITE—Southern California Back

Coach John Robinson stated, "Charlie is simply the most competitive athlete I've ever seen." Incredibly, as USC's all-purpose back, White averaged 30 to 40 carries a game. Against Notre Dame, he scored 4 touchdowns carrying 44 times and rushing for 261 yards. In his career regular season he rushed for 5,598 yards, including Bowl Games, 6,245 yards. Lifetime average 5.4 yards per carry; caught 59 passes for 541 yards, scored 53 touchdowns—a PAC 10 record. He established a total of 22 records in NCAA, PAC 10, and U.S.C.

CHARLES WHITE

1979

Card #45

This trading card was signed by former tailback Charles White, who finished his USC career as a Heisman Trophy winner and one of the game's top rushers.

These two game jerseys were worn and signed by Marv Goux, who played linebacker in the '50s but was better known as a longtime assistant coach.

USC vs. IOWA October 2, 1976 S1

JOHN ROBINSON: a Tradionalist, Motivator and Teacher

John Robinson, depicted on the cover of this 1976 game program, had two coaching stints with USC.

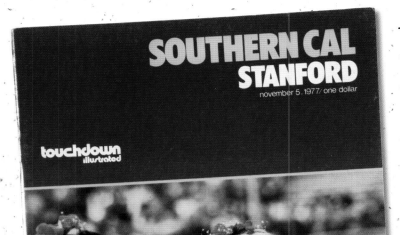

SOUTHERN CAL STANFORD

november 5, 1977/ one dollar

touchdown illustrated

The song girls grace the cover of this 1977 game program. USC swamped Stanford, their old-time rival from the north, 49–0, on the way to a victory over Texas A&M in the Bluebonnet Bowl that season.

A ticket to the 1976 Notre Dame game. The Trojans were in the midst of a three-game winning streak in this hallowed rivalry.

USC NOTRE DAME FIGHTING IRISH
SAT. NOV. 27, 1976 • 1:30 PM
L.A. COLISEUM
ESTABLISHED PRICE
$10.00
DIR. TICKET SALES

TUNNEL	ROW	SEAT
5	37	11

The Sporting News

NOVEMBER 10, 1979   PRICE: $1.25

NFL Scouts See Thin College Crop

Canadiens Plug Goalie Gap

PAUL McDONALD
Trojan Pass Master

A game ball from the 1985 Rose Bowl between No. 18 USC and No. 6 Ohio State. The Trojans pulled off a 20–17 upset victory that day.

After a stellar USC career, as noted on this issue of *The Sporting News*, McDonald was drafted by the Cleveland Browns.

Three Roses in a Row

It was supposed to be the first college football game played in the Soviet Union, a match-up between USC and Illinois called the "Glasnost Bowl," but the 1989 sea-

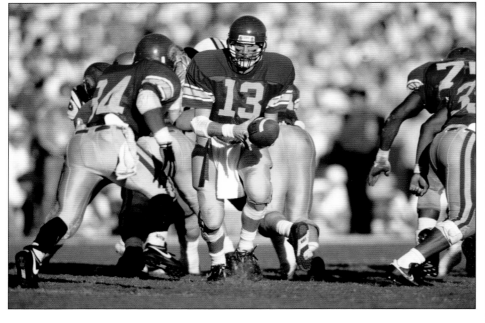

Todd Marinovich got the nickname "Robo QB" because his father raised him to play quarterback. He led the Trojans to one of three straight Rose Bowls in the late 1980s.

son opener got switched back to Los Angeles because of contract difficulties with the organizers. "It would have been a historic occasion," coach Larry Smith told the *Los Angeles Times*. "But what the heck. Nothing ventured, nothing gained." The Trojans settled for only one trip to Moscow that fall: They stayed in a Moscow, Idaho, hotel for their game across the border at Washington State.

Smith had his program on a roll. Coming off two consecutive Rose Bowl appearances, he entered 1989 with another talented squad. Most of the attention focused on freshman quarterback Todd Marinovich, dubbed "Robo

QB" because his father, former USC lineman Marv, had literally raised him to play football. As an infant, Todd had exercised in the crib and teethed on frozen chunks of kidney. As a teenager, he had followed a training regimen modeled after Soviet Bloc methods. "Through it all," he once said, "[my father] did everything he could and used all his resources to help me reach a goal."

This football is signed by the members of USC's 25th team to attend the Rose Bowl.

Marinovich suffered from the usual freshman mistakes, but he still completed more than 62 percent of his passes for 2,578 yards and 16 touchdowns. He got help from tailback Ricky Ervins and a stingy defense. The Trojans lost to Illinois and Notre Dame but swept through the conference and eked out a 10–10 tie against rival UCLA, which paved the way for their return to the Rose Bowl to face third-ranked Michigan.

Special teams gave USC a lead on New Year's Day with a blocked punt that Marinovich soon converted into a touchdown. Michigan came back to tie the score but neither team could move the ball effectively. It was left to Ervins, who grew up nearby and once parked cars outside the stadium, to provide the last-minute heroics. His 14-yard touchdown run gave USC a 17–10 win and earned him MVP honors. That day also marked Larry Smith's finest moment—he would be fired just three years later. "We felt like we had put things together," said John Jackson, who led the team in receiving with 56 yards. "We expected to win the Pac-10 championship every season, and I give Larry Smith a lot of credit."

Changing Face of Trojan Football

No story about Ronnie Lott would be complete without mentioning his pinkie. That little finger is a big part of his folklore.

Several years after leaving USC, Lott was playing defensive back for the San Francisco 49ers and mangled his finger in a late-season game. Doctors gave him a choice: He could undergo surgery and spend months in rehab or have the fingertip amputated. He told them to cut it off.

Fans who knew him from his college days were not surprised. Playing for the Trojans in the late 1970s, Lott combined brute physicality with grit and surprising athleticism. He became the benchmark in an era of USC defensive stars, with two-time All-American Tim McDonald, Thorpe Award–winner Mark Carrier, and Cleveland Colter following him in the secondary. The Trojans also fielded a succession of top linebackers in Chip Banks, Jack Del Rio, Duane Bickett, and Junior Seau.

On the offensive side of the ball, the tailback position faded from the limelight after Marcus Allen won the Heisman Trophy in 1981. It was time for the passing game to take over as the Trojans featured one All-America receiver after another. Erik Affholter started the streak in 1988 and was soon followed by Curtis Conway and Johnnie Morton. Big, brash Keyshawn Johnson earned MVP honors with his record performances in both the 1995 Cotton Bowl and 1996 Rose Bowl.

Those guys needed someone to throw them the ball, so quarterbacks also gained more prominence. Not long after

All-American Ronnie Lott led the way for a procession of defensive stars at USC in the 1980s.

Paul McDonald finished a sterling college career, Rodney Peete took over as a freshman and led USC to four consecutive bowl games. Though he set a school record with 8,225 career-passing yards, Peete will always be remembered for one of his worst throws.

The Trojans were losing 10–0 against UCLA in 1987. Peete was driving his team toward a score with seconds remaining in the first half when he threw an interception just short of the end zone. The Bruin defender sprinted along the sideline for almost 90 yards before Peete somehow caught him. The saving tackle made all the difference as USC charged back in the second half to win 17–13.

Sports Illustrated believed that Keyshawn Johnson would be a force for USC in 1995.

The Coliseum Gets a Face-Lift

An earthquake that shook Los Angeles in early 1994 caused major damage to the aging Coliseum.

Much was changing in the early 1990s. The Trojans turned to a new coach, hoping to recapture their glory years. A new tailback was carrying the ball. The stadium they played in went through a major transformation.

Ever since the days of the 1932 Summer Olympics, fans coming to watch football at the Coliseum had been separated from players by a running track that encircled the field. Prior to the 1993 season, the stadium commission approved a $15-million renovation. The track was removed and the field lowered by almost a dozen feet, making room for 14 rows of seats that extended to within 50 or so feet of the sideline. Metal bleachers were added directly behind the east end zone. "The seats used to start pretty far out there," said Pat Lynch, the stadium's general manager. "It brought the fans closer to the football action."

But the improved Coliseum lasted only a few months—enough for one season—before a major earthquake struck Southern California, causing widespread damage across the region. The stadium was hit hard. Workers began with repairs in spring, racing to finish before the Trojans and their cotenant, the Los Angeles Raiders of the NFL, returned the next fall. Workers excavated the concourse and reinforced beams that supported the upper sections, along with buttressing the famous peristyle arches. Concession stands, once dug into the earthen berm around the outside of the bowl, had to be moved into small, free-standing buildings. The final price tag? Almost $100 million.

"We started in April and had to be done by September," said Lynch. "At that time, luckily, neither the Raiders nor USC were drawing huge crowds, so it was doable."

Bird's-Eye View

By the end of summer, the Coliseum was repaired and ready for a new football season—almost. The commission had to patch together a temporary press box for sportswriters, assistant coaches, and others who watched the games from a perch high above the field. Not that any of these people missed the old box, which was torn down after the earthquake. "It was narrow," general manager Pat Lynch said. "It was tight."

The following spring, the commission paid $6 million for a new, multi-story structure along the stadium's southern rim. Coaches, broadcasters, and sportswriters now had room to move around. University officials and boosters could spend their Saturday afternoons in suites on the lower levels. "Night and day," Lynch said. "The new one was a lot nicer."

Return of the Fat Man

John Robinson returned to USC in 1993, inheriting a program that had fallen short of expectations after his 1982 departure. He soon had the team winning again.

There wasn't anything complicated about the decision to bring back John Robinson. When the university announced his return in the winter of 1993, President Steven B. Sample told reporters that he embodied "a reassertion of the Trojan tradition." After all, this was a man who had guided the team to three Rose Bowls and a national championship in the late 1970s.

Robinson was a popular choice with fans and the media, very personable and quick to joke. His résumé now included a successful stint with the Los Angeles Rams, as well as a year in the television booth. More importantly, he vowed to revive the tradition of the power tailback that had faded under the previous USC coach, Larry Smith. As Robinson explained years later: "We didn't want to go away from the run-first thing."

Not that the program could be transformed overnight. With no Charles White or Marcus Allen waiting on the roster, the Trojans stumbled through much of the 1993 season, losing four games on the road and dropping a heartbreaker to UCLA on a last-second interception in the end zone. Their 7–5 record sent them to the less-than-glamorous Freedom Bowl. But where previous teams had faltered in minor bowl games, losing to lesser opponents, USC defeated Utah 28–21 to end the season on an optimistic note.

Progress continued the following year thanks mainly to a new receiver named Keyshawn Johnson, whose size and strength were matched only by a larger-than-life personality. The Trojans strung together five victories at midseason and scored in the final minutes to tie Notre Dame, ending an 11-year losing streak to their intersectional rival. Invited to play Texas Tech in the Cotton Bowl, they cruised to a 55–14 victory as Johnson had a career day with 222 receiving yards and three touchdowns.

If there was a growing sense of nostalgia around the program, it wasn't only because of Robinson; another familiar face roamed Heritage Hall. Just weeks after the old coach was rehired, Sample promoted former Heisman Trophy–winning tailback Mike Garrett to the position of athletic director. "It's a very simple mission for me," Garrett was quoted as saying in the *Los Angeles Times*. "And that is, just be 'SC." The Trojan football tradition appeared to be in good hands.

In January 1993, USC named a familiar figure, former tailback Mike Garrett, as athletic director.

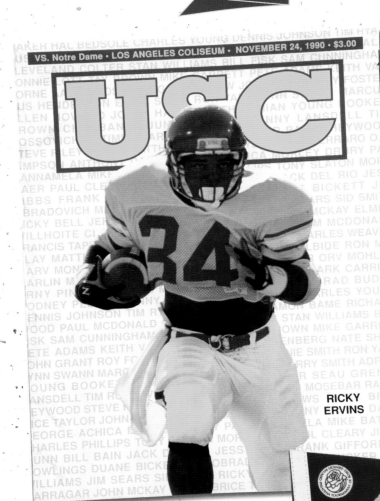

A stellar offensive tackle, John Michels celebrates with the Rose Bowl trophy in 1996.

Tickets to USC games were a hot commodity in 1978 as the Trojans won the national championship.

Tailback Ricky Ervins, on the cover of this program from the 1990 Notre Dame game, had been a Rose Bowl star a year earlier.

The 1989 season started with an upset loss to Illinois, but the Trojans improved, ultimately beating Michigan in the 1990 Rose Bowl.

A game ball from the 1982 Fiesta Bowl, where USC ran into a dominating Penn State team and lost 26–10.

THE 1977 ROSE BOWL USC vs. MICHIGAN

JANUARY 1 / PASADENA, CALIFORNIA
official souvenir program / $2

Third-ranked USC pulled off an upset at the 1977 Rose Bowl with a 14–6 win over second-ranked Michigan.

The Sporting News put Marcus Allen on its 1981 All-America team and on its cover.

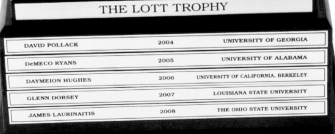

THE LOTT TROPHY		
DAVID POLLACK	2004	UNIVERSITY OF GEORGIA
DeMECO RYANS	2005	UNIVERSITY OF ALABAMA
DAYMEION HUGHES	2006	UNIVERSITY OF CALIFORNIA, BERKELEY
GLENN DORSEY	2007	LOUISIANA STATE UNIVERSITY
JAMES LAURINAITIS	2008	THE OHIO STATE UNIVERSITY

A trophy named after Ronnie Lott is awarded to college football's top defensive player each season.

The Road to Pasadena

As USC embarked on the third year of "John Robinson II," most of the players recruited by the previous coach, Larry Smith, were gone and expectations ran high. Maybe too high, Robinson worried. But coming off a big Cotton Bowl victory, he could not quiet the talk of a return to glory days.

Making good on that promise would not be easy. The 1995 season began with star receiver Keyshawn Johnson under NCAA scrutiny for allegedly receiving a loan from an agent while in junior college. As those charges faded, others cropped up. Three top players, including tailback Shawn Walters, were suspended for taking cash from yet another agent. Despite such chaos, USC managed to win its first six games by convincing scores.

Two quarterbacks led the Trojans through the early season, Brad Otton playing the first and third quarters, with Kyle Wachholtz replacing him in the second and fourth. LaVale Woods led the way at tailback before Delon Washington stepped in. This mix-and-match offense finally hit a roadblock in late October, committing four turnovers in a 38–10 loss to Notre Dame.

It was a defeat that almost derailed the season. USC visited Washington the next week and started so poorly that the usually calm Robinson laid into his players at halftime. Otton sparked a comeback, staying in the game through the fourth quarter and guiding his team to three touchdowns for an important tie. The Trojans fell to UCLA in the regular-season finale—their fifth consecutive stumble in the crosstown rivalry—but by that time they had clinched a trip to Pasadena.

Their opponent on New Year's Day was third-ranked Northwestern, a Cinderella team playing in its first Rose Bowl since just after World War II. In a wild game, the Trojans sprinted to a halftime lead only to fall behind in the fourth quarter. It took a couple of Wildcat turnovers—one controversial—and a pair of late scores for USC to earn a 41–32 victory. Otton played an entire game for the first time that season, passing for 391 yards, and Washington finished the season as the program's first 1,000-yard tailback in five years. The star of the day was Johnson, with a Rose Bowl–record 216 receiving yards and a critical touchdown. Northwestern Coach Gary Barnett mused: "Keyshawn? He must have caught 100 passes."

For much of the 1995 season, Brad Otton (above) alternated at quarterback with Kyle Wachholtz. Eventually, Otton took command and led USC to a 41–32 victory over Northwestern in the Rose Bowl.

Big and strong for a receiver, Keyshawn Johnson manhandled the Northwestern defense in the 1996 Rose Bowl.

Working Overtime

The fall of 1996 brought historic change to college football with the adoption of an overtime system for games ending in a tie. This wasn't like professional football, where the first score won. The NCAA rules committee devised an elaborate procedure by which each team got an offensive series beginning at the opponent's 25-yard line, trying to score a touchdown or at least a field goal. This back-and-forth repeated until one team came out on top.

The Trojans wasted little time testing the system, playing in no less than three overtime games that season.

Their first experience came on an October day in the desert. USC opened a lead but the defense wilted, allowing Arizona State to tie the game with less than two minutes remaining. Both teams scored in the first overtime, then the Sun Devils took a 42–35 lead in the second. That's when the officials got involved. Earlier in the game, they had awarded USC a touchdown on a play in which receiver Chris Miller appeared to drop the ball. Now, they ruled that Brad Otton's incomplete shovel pass was a fumble, recovered by Arizona State and returned for a touchdown to end the game at 48–35. "We went head-to-head with them for a long time," USC defensive tackle Darrell Russell told the *Los Angeles Times*. "And one of us slipped."

If that defeat stung, it was nothing compared to the UCLA game several weeks later. The Trojans seemed ready to break a five-year winless streak against their rivals when, once again, they faltered late and let the Bruins rally from 17 points down. Both teams scored in the first overtime,

but on the second go-around UCLA tailback Skip Hicks raced for a touchdown and the Trojans could not answer; quarterback Matt Koffler's pass was intercepted in the end zone to seal a 48–41 loss. The defeat ruined a record-setting day for R. Jay Soward, who had 260 receiving yards and three touchdowns.

The Trojans got it right on their third try. Playing against Notre Dame at the Coliseum, they came back from eight points down, scored in the first extra session, and batted away a fourth-down pass to score a 27–20 victory. After 13 long years, USC finally had a win against the Irish. Now the other side knew the pain of losing in overtime; Notre Dame Coach Lou Holtz said: "I feel like somebody reached into my stomach and pulled out my guts."

Rodney Sermons breaks free against Notre Dame as the Trojans come back to defeat the Irish in overtime. The 1996 victory ended USC's 13-year winless streak in the grand rivalry.

An Unfortunate Ending

One victory shy of his 100th win—a prestigious mark for any college coach—John Robinson wasn't thinking about his place in the record books. He was too busy trying to get the Trojans back on track. They were coming off a mediocre season and had dropped two of their first three in the fall of 1997. The experts cast them as heavy favorites against Nevada-Las Vegas in early October, but no game felt like a sure thing anymore. "You're always trying to win this week, then win the next week," Robinson told the *Los Angeles Times*. "It's kind of a funny deal."

The coach got his landmark victory against UNLV at the Coliseum, his team scoring three straight touchdowns in the fourth quarter, but that did not quiet growing concerns. During Robinson's first stint at USC, he had been celebrated for his enthusiasm.

As former quarterback Paul McDonald recalled: "He got in the middle of things. He used to show the offensive linemen how to block." Now critics sensed a change. The beloved "fat man" did not seem as energetic this time around, nor did his staff measure up to the previous one, which had included future head coaches Norv Turner and Bob Toledo. Past glories seemed all too distant as the Trojans hovered near .500, the end of an illustrious career looming ever closer.

In the final weeks of the season, news broke that athletic director Mike Garrett was considering various options. Garrett offered the job to Robinson's former assistant Paul Hackett, but he couldn't reach Robinson by phone, so he left a message on his answering machine. The next day, USC held one news conference on campus while the dismissed coach held another at a downtown hotel. University president Steven B. Sample said Robinson had agreed to resign, which wasn't the case. There were tense words from both sides and from alumni and players who felt an honored Trojan had been mistreated.

Lonnie White, the receiver who wrote the book *UCLA vs. USC: 75 Years of the Greatest Rivalry in Sports*, said: "He was passionate, and he was a great motivator. You always felt that he wanted to be out there playing with you."

USC's firing of John Robinson in 1997 turned messy when the school held one news conference on campus and Robinson held his own at a nearby hotel.

The 1997 season wasn't all bad for USC coach John Robinson. After the Trojans defeated Nevada-Las Vegas at the Coliseum in early October, he got the chance to celebrate his 100th collegiate victory.

A Roller-Coaster Ride

For USC, the seasons that spanned from 1976 through 1997 were filled with highs and lows. Fans endured stadium renovations, a major earthquake, and more renovations. At a school where the likes of Howard Jones and John McKay had become fixtures, they watched no fewer than five coaching changes. They sat quietly as Washington ended their team's record unbeaten streak in the fall of 1980, then cheered wildly when USC defeated Notre Dame in the Coliseum's first overtime game in 1996.

This era saw the Trojans gradually fade from the national championship picture and attendance dwindle. Instead of 60,000 to 70,000 on Saturday afternoons, the average crowd now dropped into the 50,000 range. Rivalry games still packed the stadium, but it was impossible to maintain that level of excitement for Oregon State and Arizona.

The passing years took their toll on other traditions. Card stunts, which had debuted at USC in 1922, were temporarily banned in the early 1990s. University adminis-

trators were concerned about fan safety because students kept flinging the heavy cards into the air. Sporadic attempts to revive the stunts failed, and they eventually became a dim memory. Even Traveler had to adapt as the running track was removed from around the field. With less room to gallop along the sidelines, the horse and its rider bumped a rival cheerleader and had to be more careful.

There were other changes at the Coliseum. The Los Angeles Rams moved out following the 1979 season, and a couple of years later so did UCLA. No longer did cross-town rivals share the same field. Both teams donned their home jerseys—cardinal against blue—in the annual game for one more year until a rule was enacted requiring the visitor to wear white.

Around that time, the Coliseum underwent another round of remodeling prompted by the 1984 Summer Olympics. The stadium got its own version of Tommy Trojan, a pair of nude, headless statues outside the peristyle end, reportedly modeled after Olympic athletes Terry Schroeder of the United States and Jennifer Innes of Guyana. The Trojans continued to share their home with the Los Angeles Raiders and, for a short time, with the Los Angeles Express of the USFL. By the mid-1990s, they had the place to themselves.

By the 1970s, the USC song girls had become a symbol of the football program with their crisp white sweaters and matching skirts.

When the running track was removed from around the Coliseum field, Traveler and his rider had to take care not to trample rival cheerleaders on the sideline.

UCLA: Too Close for Comfort

USC's Johnnie Morton catches a Todd Marinovich pass to defeat UCLA 45–42 in the 1990 edition of the crosstown rivalry.

There is an old saying that familiarity breeds contempt—and that might go a long way toward explaining USC's relationship with UCLA. The universities stand about 14 miles apart, so players are bound to run into each other at the movies and at restaurants. "You really learn to hate UCLA when you lose to them," said quarterback Carson Palmer. "It's just having to go through a whole year of them talking." The campuses are close enough for students to conduct crosstown raids.

read "USC" during the game. Adversaries have printed and distributed fake copies of each other's campus newspapers. In 1989, USC students released hundreds of crickets into a UCLA library during finals week. This back-and-forth doesn't end with graduation.

Rival alumni and fans work in the same offices, live next door to each other, and even marry. So it is no surprise when a city councilman crows about his team during public hearings or a downtown salesman loses a bet on the game and must stand on his desk in women's underwear, singing the other school's fight song. When a San Fernando Valley doctor finds his consultation room festooned with cardinal-and-gold balloons, he knows to blame the pharmacist downstairs. Of course, none of this would be possible without the games.

The Trojans, already an established football power by the time UCLA came along, dominated the early years until the Bruins developed into a top-notch program in the 1960s, which is when the rivalry heated up. Two games, in particular, attracted national attention. First, UCLA quarterback Gary Beban threw a 52-yard bomb with 2 minutes 39 seconds remaining to give his team a 20–16 victory in 1965. Then came O. J. Simpson's 64-yard run and a 21–20 win for the Trojans two years later.

Beating UCLA meant everything to John McKay, who quite possibly saved his job with an upset victory over the Bruins in his first year as head coach. His assistants noticed that he would grow more animated as the big game approached. On the practice field, where he often

From the beginning, the USC rivalry with UCLA has been intense, as evidenced by this special program from 1967.

The history of pranks extends far beyond mere splashing of blue paint on Tommy Trojan. In the 1950s, Bruin students reportedly rented a helicopter and dropped 500 pounds of manure on the famed statue. The Trojans answered by covertly rigging a UCLA card stunt so that it

shuttled between drills in a golf cart, the coach was more likely to jump out and walk among his players. As for motivational speeches, quarterback Pat Haden said, "it was one of those games you didn't have to talk about." Years later, after his retirement, McKay confided to a friend: "You know what? I'd find a way to win that game. I don't care if I lost all the rest of them, I'd focus on that one."

The battles continued after he left. The Trojans prevailed with a last-second field goal in 1977, and the Bruins came right back in 1980 when tailback Freeman McNeil caught a deflected pass—tipped by USC defensive back and future NFL coach Jeff Fisher—for a game-winning touchdown in the final minutes. The Trojans blocked a field-goal attempt to preserve a victory in 1981. The Bruins disrupted a two-point conversion attempt to hang on the next year.

But for all these memories, perhaps nothing could match what happened in 1990 when a tight contest turned wild at the end. The teams raced back and forth across the field, scoring no less than six touchdowns in the fourth quarter, three of them in the final three minutes and nine seconds. The Trojans' mercurial quarterback, Todd Marinovich, finally settled matters with 16 seconds remaining, firing a 23-yard touchdown pass to Johnnie Morton to give USC a 45–42 victory.

After that win, the Trojans lost eight straight years to UCLA—an eternity for fans—before rebounding with a winning streak of their own. They prevailed in eight of the next nine meetings, their only loss coming in 2006 when they fell to unranked UCLA 13–9, losing a berth in the national championship game. It was the kind of surprise that coaches, players, and fans have come to expect from this rivalry. "It's a game where both teams just let it go," said Rick Neuheisel, a UCLA quarterback in the early 1980s who later became coach of the Bruins. "Some strange things have happened."

USC quarterback Todd Marinovich looks for a hole in the UCLA defense during the 1990 game. No other rivalries in major college football match teams that must share a city for the rest of the year.

MICHIGAN vs. USC

CHARLES WHITE

RICK LEACH

65th ROSE BOWL
January 1, 1979

The media receive special guides, such as this one from the 1979 Rose Bowl, packed with statistics.

Charles White finished his college career with a Pac-10 record 6,245 yards (including bowl games). He gained 100 yards in a game 31 times in his college career. In 1979, he won the Heisman Trophy.

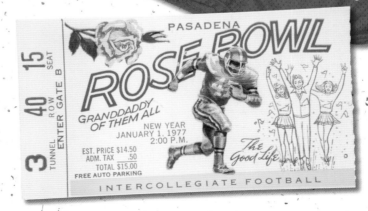

PASADENA

ROSE BOWL

GRANDDADDY OF THEM ALL

NEW YEAR
JANUARY 1, 1977
2:00 P.M.

EST. PRICE $14.50
ADM. TAX   .50
TOTAL $15.00
FREE AUTO PARKING

The Good Life

INTERCOLLEGIATE FOOTBALL

TUNNEL 3   ROW 40   ENTER GATE B   SEAT 15

This ticket to the 1977 Rose Bowl game bears the theme "The Good Life" from that year's Rose Parade.

A game ball signed by the 1979 Rose Bowl players is a special piece of memorabilia.

Players receive various mementos for appearing in the Rose Bowl. This ring is from the 1996 game.

Sports Illustrated

ROLLING BACK THE TIDE

USC's Charles White

$1.25

Tailback Charles White darts through a hole against Alabama and makes the cover of Sports Illustrated.

U.C.L.A. vs U.S.C. Nov. 21, 1981

This pennant was made specially for the 1981 crosstown rivalry played at the Coliseum.

Return to Glory

1998–Today

After two decades of near misses and no national championships, a savior arrives at USC. The energetic and upbeat Pete Carroll leads the program back to the future, reviving a lost tradition of big bowl victories. Along the way, the Trojans fielded three Heisman Trophy winners in Carson Palmer, Matt Leinart, and Reggie Bush.

With fireworks bursting in the night sky, the Trojans take the field to play Oklahoma for the 2005 national title, a game that marked their return to the top of the college football world.

Tailback Joe McKnight slashes through the Penn State defense in the 2009 Rose Bowl, leading the Trojans to another victory in Pasadena.

A Walk Through History

When players describe the shabby corridor that runs under the Coliseum stands, they talk about ghosts. They mention the darkness and the sounds that bounce off the concrete walls. Words such as "thrilling" and "historic" come up. Sometimes even "sacred."

College football has no shortage of landmarks, from the glistening Touchdown Jesus at Notre Dame to the English privet hedges that line the field at Georgia. But for the Trojans, nothing could be more special than the dank corridor that connects their locker room to the field. Walking this short passage has become a ritual that marks the beginning of each home game, with shadows leading into dazzling brightness. "There's 90,000 people screaming and the band playing," linebacker Dallas Sartz said. "It's a tremendous feeling."

Longtime assistant Marv Goux played to the folklore of the tunnel, leading his players to the opening and hold-

In their home at the Coliseum, the Trojans use the anxious moments before kickoff to gather as a team and get revved up, then they charge onto the field.

ing them just short of the turf until they grew sufficiently agitated. "You'd better not be in front unless you were one of those guys ready to rip and scream onto the field," said Hal Bedsole, an All-America receiver from the early 1960s. "I was never one of those guys, so my years at 'SC, I was the last one out."

The importance of this tradition struck home with Bedsole in 1963, when Ohio State visited the Coliseum. Coach John McKay expressed outrage when he saw the Buckeyes walking casually out of the tunnel. "He gave us an enormous pre-game speech," Bedsole recalled. "He'd never done that. He said 'We're not letting them walk onto our field like that.'"

Paul Cleary, an All-American in 1947, went a step further when he spoke of the tunnel in metaphysical terms after suffering a heart attack in 1978. Cleary described a classic near-death experience, seeing a bright light in the darkness, except his vision came with a twist. "In my mind,

I was coming out of the Los Angeles Coliseum dressing room, through the tunnel and onto the field," he said.

The walk begins at the locker-room door, 50 or so yards from the field. Because of the tunnel's long downward curve, the team cannot see the field at the other end and the only illumination comes from dim fixtures on the wall. Players say the short journey can feel like it takes forever and surprisingly little noise seeps in from the stadium, so the cavernous space fills with echoes of cleats rattling across the concrete floor. "It's kind of like the tradition of a gladiator," quarterback Mike Rae said. "Everybody's keyed up, and you have this image of walking to war, more or less." Not until the final few yards does the team emerge into a blare of emotion. "You hear the fans and see that light," defensive tackle Sedrick Ellis said. "You're almost on the field, and they hold you up."

Over the years, USC coaches have used this trick as a recruiting tool. They escort high school prospects through the tunnel, into the sudden daylight for dramatic effect. It sold quarterback Todd Marinovich, who recalled that "when I walked down the tunnel at the Coliseum, I knew." Even visiting players have felt something special. "When you walk through the tunnel . . . you [realize] the Super Bowl's been here and they've had the Olympics here," Penn State linebacker Keith Goganious told the *Los Angeles Times* after his team played USC in 1990. "You just feel the magic that's in that stadium."

Not all the folklore surrounding the tunnel is uplifting. Coach John Robinson slipped coming onto the field in 1976, and legend holds that in the 1950s a player fell and

was inadvertently trampled by teammates, breaking his leg. Because both teams share the passageway, officials sometimes struggle to keep the competitors separated. Linebacker Sam Anno recalled a game in the mid-1980s when the Trojans and Notre Dame got into "a full-on fight. Probably 40 or 50 guys pushing." During losing seasons, coaches and players walking back to the locker room have been subjected to abuse from fans leaning over the entrance.

But for the most part, the tunnel is a place of inspiration and tradition. A place where USC teams have always gathered, hopping up and down, slapping helmets beside a banner that lists all of the program's national championships and Rose Bowl appearances. A place where the team prepares for battle. As Ellis said: "You can't wait to get on the field."

Pete Carroll and his team stand at the mouth of the Coliseum tunnel, beside a banner celebrating the program's past glories. Carroll wants players to appreciate the tradition of Trojan football.

Team merchandise almost never includes the words "Southern Cal"—the school doesn't like that term.

LenDale White signed this jersey. The tailback out-rushed Reggie Bush in two of their three seasons together.

C

THE COACH

© Copyright 2000-2009   www.CoachStickers.com

Coach Pete Carroll may have been an unpopular hire at first, but his success at USC has launched an array of merchandise such as this sticker.

USC memorabilia would look far different if the school had stuck with an early nickname—the Methodists.

Fans' hunger for team merchandise has transformed college football into a profitable business. This vintage gold pin is an early example.

Matt Leinart's touchdown catch on a trick play was the signature moment of the 2004 Rose Bowl.

This album is one of several the Trojan Marching Band has produced. It features songs such as "Tribute to Troy," "Conquest," and "Fight On."

The Consummate Football Band

It was 1970 and Arthur C. Bartner had moved west from Michigan to begin a new job as USC's marching band director. He was waiting in line to eat lunch at the university commons when inspiration struck by way of a gruff assistant coach named Marv Goux. "He came up behind me and he's got this meat hook of a hand and he just grabbed me by the back of the neck," Bartner recalled. "He told me that he didn't want any wimpy band. He wanted a jock band." An unusual friendship began that day, leading to an unusual amalgam of music and football.

The Trojan Marching Band, known as "The Spirit of Troy," might seem a bit Hollywood, with its rows of musicians adorned in shiny gold helmets and sunglasses, the recording sessions with Fleetwood Mac, and guest appearances at the Academy Awards. But Goux demanded that the team come first, and Bartner responded with precise marching and a rousing musical style. The director explained: "Marv literally took me under his wing and explained to me what it meant to be a Trojan. He really set the tone for a lot of the traditions we have."

Sword in hand, quarterback John David Booty leads the Trojan Marching Band after USC's win over Illinois in the 2008 Rose Bowl. For more than three decades, there has been a strong connection between the team and the band.

Trumpets and tubas had been accompanying games since the 1880s. Through the first half-century of USC football, the band paraded in white flannel trousers and flowing gold shirts, performing traditional favorites such as "Fight On!" and "All Hail." In 1947, the university hired a new director, Clarence Sawhill, whose preference for the big band sound was a hit. But the band's popularity soared after Bartner arrived. Goux's enthusiasm inspired the New Jersey native to stretch to try something different.

"Marv wanted us to be a football band and respond to every play, to be a catalyst for spirit and energy," Bartner said. "I thought, 'Well, how do we do this?'"

The new director began to treat rehearsals like football practice, barking commands from his station, demanding that musicians perfect what he called the "drive-it" style of marching. Each step had to be exact, thigh extended to 45 degrees with toe pointed downward, back foot snapping off the ground. And Bartner devised a soundtrack for the games. "Fight On!" rang out after each first down and touchdown. Interceptions prompted a chorus of "All Right Now." And big defensive plays started the band on its most famous—or infamous—song.

From the first notes of "Tribute to Troy," USC fans thrust their hands into the air, waving the V for victory sign, while rivals cringe because the band repeats the tune as many as 50 times a game. "They know people hate that fight song, and they play it anyway," California running back Russell White once told the *Seattle Post-Intelligencer.*

The Trojan Marching Band has built an international reputation by performing at four Super Bowls, a World Series, and two Olympic Games. It has been a part of three World Expos, the New Year in Hong Kong, and a handful of movies, including *Hello Dolly.* But Bartner never forgot that thick hand on the back of his neck. "Marv wanted a football band," he said. "I think that's what he got."

Star Power

How many college marching bands can say they have paraded onto the field with Stevie Nicks as majorette? And played the trumpet fanfare at a papal mass? And accompanied the hip-hop duo Outkast on stage?

Much like the USC football program has deep ties with Hollywood, the Trojan Marching Band has performed duets with a list of conductors and musicians as varied and famous as any Grammy Awards lineup, including Henry Mancini, Quincy Jones, Chuck Mangione, Leonard Bernstein, Diana Ross, and Neil Diamond. Its members have appeared in various movies, including *Forrest Gump* and *The Naked Gun.*

Perhaps the band's greatest moment came in 1979 when it played on the title track of Fleetwood Mac's platinum-selling album *Tusk.* That session turned into a friendship that saw the unlikely partners perform together on stage and the field. In the fourth game of the 1980 season, lead singer Nicks twirled "The Spirit of Troy" through a halftime routine at the Coliseum.

Parliament-Funkadelic's George Clinton with the USC band.

The Quarterbacks' Guru

Paul Hackett, in happier times, cheers USC's victory over Penn State in 2000.

The transition from John Robinson to a new coach was anything but seamless. First came the mess of Robinson's firing with its miscommunications, dueling press conferences, and hurt feelings. Then the university hired a replacement, Paul Hackett, who was still busy preparing for the NFL playoffs as the Kansas City Chiefs' offensive coordinator. A month passed before he took over.

Hackett was familiar to Trojan fans; he served as one of Robinson's top assistants from 1976 to 1980. The football world knew him as a devotee of the West Coast offense and a quarterback's guru, the man who nurtured Joe Montana with the 49ers. There were questions about his prospects as a head coach—his only previous attempt at the University of Pittsburgh had lasted only three seasons. With his big glasses and the way he tugged a ball cap down over his head, critics viewed him as more of a technician than a leader. But Hackett knew the program and brought a jolt of enthusiasm, telling reporters it was "an honor and a privilege to be the head coach at USC.... I'm jacked up."

The 1998 season began with an emotional victory followed by unexpected losses in conference. The Trojans fell to UCLA, beat Notre Dame, then lost in an upset to Texas Christian at the Sun Bowl to finish 8–5. From this mixed start, things quickly went downhill.

Hackett never got a grip on special teams, and his offense might have been too complex for the college game. Fans grumbled when the Trojans seemed to gain momentum but chose to play it safe, running instead of passing, punting instead of gambling on fourth down. In Hackett's second season, injuries contributed to a five-game losing streak at midseason, with the team finishing 6–6. He swore that things would get better: But the 2000 season turned out even worse. A fast start gave way to another five-game losing streak and a 5–7 record, and the grumbles turned to boos. While Carson Palmer supported his coach, other players didn't. Receiver Kareem Kelly said: "A lot of guys want him back. There's also a lot of guys who don't care."

Three and Out

The end came slow and sure, Notre Dame pounding away at the USC defense, scoring the final ten points to break open a close game. A 38–21 loss sent the Trojans home with a 5–7 record for the 2000 season and increased the heat on their embattled coach. In a postgame news conference, Paul Hackett talked like a man who wanted to stick around, making references to the next fall and the problems that needed solving. Asked if he deserved to come back, he bristled: "Are you out of your mind? Of course I do."

But the next day, athletic director Mike Garrett told the coach he was fired. A gracious Hackett acknowledged that his predictions for a successful third season had been overly ambitious. "These are the things you calculate as a coach," he said. "You think you can overcome them. Sometimes you do and sometimes you don't." Meanwhile, sources within the athletic department said Garrett had already prepared a list of potential replacements.

Super Fan

The game itself wasn't noteworthy, not with the Trojans cruising to a 74–0 victory in their season opener against Whittier. But that late September day in 1926 marked the beginning of something extraordinary in the stands: an amazing streak for a fan named Giles Pellerin.

An engineering student at the time, Pellerin did not miss another USC game, home or away, for the next 72 years. That stretch encompassed 797 games, including 28 Rose Bowls and the first 69 installments of the Notre Dame rivalry. He watched almost a dozen different coaches and 121 All-Americans come and go, spending upward of $85,000 to traverse more than 650,000 miles, attending road games in more than 50 cities. "Some people think I'm crazy for spending as much money as I have traveling to see these games," he once said. Saturday afternoons meant something more than touchdowns and tackles for the phone company executive who predated both Tommy Trojan and Traveler. He talked about people he met and places he visited. "I never played the game, but I love it," he said. "There's just a certain spirit about college football."

Keeping the streak alive wasn't easy. There were lost tickets and broken-down cars along the way. Recuperating from an emergency appendectomy in 1949, Pellerin told nurses that he was going for a walk but instead snuck out to the game. In 1993, he had to sign a liability waiver to gain early release from yet another hospital so he could watch the Trojans play Washington State.

Finally, during the second half of the 1998 UCLA game, the 91-year-old Pellerin left the Rose Bowl feeling ill and suffered a cardiac arrest in the parking lot. Friends said he died doing something he loved. As Pellerin had explained earlier: "I've always said that going to USC games is the thing that has kept me alive, young, and happy."

> "I've always said that going to USC games is the thing that has kept me alive, young, and happy."
>
> **Giles Pellerin**

Above: *Pellerin (right), in 1977, talks with Kennedy B. Galpin, a USC trustee, and his wife, Barbara.*
Left: *Pellerin attended the Notre Dame game in 1932—only five years into his streak.*

Rituals and Routines

For Trojan fans, going to the game means partaking in a series of rituals that begins with tailgate parties on campus and continues inside the stadium. The USC student section adds color to the crowd at the Coliseum.

As game time approaches, a clanging sound rings across the southern edge of campus. One after another, fans strolling from the university toward the Coliseum make sure to kick the bases of several flagpoles along the way. This simple if noisy act is supposed to bring the team luck—just one of the many rituals and routines surrounding USC football.

Saturday afternoons begin with tailgate parties that range from catered to informal, a mass of tables, lawn chairs, and blankets arranged beside the library, under trees at Taper Hall, and all around the stadium. Two hours before kickoff, hundreds of rooters gather outside the peristyle end of the Coliseum for a custom that coach Pete Carroll established in 2001. Carroll wanted his players to appreciate their home field, so he had them get off the team bus and cover the last few hundred yards on foot.

"Walking into the Coliseum is a very special experience," he said. "I want them to see that." Word quickly spread, and with each game more and more fans lined the so-called "Trojan Walk," cheering as the team passes. "You can't help but feed off the energy," receiver Patrick Turner said. "The fans feel like they can pour their hearts out."

Tradition continues inside the stadium with a drum major in shining gold breastplate who strides to the 50-yard line and buries his sword in the turf. The band strikes up "Tribute to Troy" for the first of many times, and fans raise their hands into the air, waving the two-fingered V for victory sign. According to legend, this gesture dates back to longbowmen who fought for England in the Hundred Years War and was later popularized by Winston Churchill. No one seems to know when or how USC adopted the V, but it has become an indelible part of the team's folklore.

There are other rituals, fans calling for "The Horse!," singing in falsetto to the flute part in "Conquest," and screaming their way through the "So-Cal Spell Out." The day ends with a stadium full of people swaying to the music of "All Hail." As Carroll once said of USC: "I grew up watching the tradition, watching the Rose Bowl, watching the UCLA and Notre Dame games at the end of the season. I always loved the spectacle of it."

In helmet and shining breastplate, the Trojan drum major strides to the 50-yard line and plunges his sword into the turf.

What Could Have Been

The play looked simple, Carson Palmer scrambling under pressure, running toward the sideline in the final minute before halftime. The big quarterback—he stood 6'5", 220 pounds—lowered his shoulder into a smaller defender and bounced out of bounds for a 3-yard gain. No one in the stands heard the crunch, the sound of Palmer's collarbone snapping. "One second changed my life," he said later. "I couldn't believe what happened." He was done for the night, and all hell was about to break loose.

A raucous second half. No less than three overtimes. By the time it was over, USC's visit to Autzen Stadium early in the 1999 season would rank as the longest and perhaps strangest game in school history.

At first, Palmer's injury appeared to swing the momentum firmly toward Oregon, with the Ducks taking control in the third quarter. But USC's second-string quarterback, Mike Van Raaphorst, gradually found his rhythm, leading the team on a pair of fourth-quarter drives. When tailback Chad Morton reached the end zone with 3:08 remaining, giving USC the lead, his teammates went wild. So wild, in fact, officials penalized them for excessive celebration and they missed the extra point, leaving the score 23–20. USC had another opportunity to put the game away but missed a field goal. "It's a protection issue, a snapping issue, a kicking issue," Coach Paul Hackett said. "I think it's an Astroturf issue and an Oregon issue, because it is noisy." Oregon was able to tie the game in the waning moments.

Both teams failed to score in the first overtime. Both had touchdowns in the second. By then, the Ducks were relegated to their reserve kickers because it turned out the

starter had injured himself celebrating the field goal at the end of regulation. In the third overtime, USC's David Newbury missed a third-consecutive kick and Oregon third-stringer Josh Frankel was good from 27 yards. A swarm of Duck fans rushed the field. Hackett mourned "what could have been a magnificent victory in a hostile environment," was a game that turned into "a devastating loss."

USC safety Ifeanyi Ohalete chases an Oregon ballcarrier during the 1999 game in which Carson Palmer broke his collarbone.

The Right Man for the Job

The Coliseum stood dark and empty, football season long over, as the USC players arrived for an unexpected night meeting. They had been summoned to the stadium by their new coach, Pete Carroll, who delivered a speech on teamwork, then he broke them into groups for a tug-of-war. Offensive lineman Lenny Vandermade recalled thinking: *This is something new.*

The Trojans soon grew accustomed to their frenetic young leader, a guy who dove into the pile during goal-line drills, staged elaborate Halloween pranks, and interrupted practices for impromptu swim parties. They also got used to winning.

Beginning with his first season in 2001, Carroll guided the team to eight consecutive bowl games—including four straight Rose Bowls—and two national championships. This success ranked him among such hallowed names as Howard Jones and John McKay, even if he did not fit the mold of the traditional coach. "That can be a great way to teach, but it's not me," he explained. "I get more out of you if I connect with you. Instead of knocking you down and challenging you to come back up, I'm going to build you."

His unconventional approach dated back to the University of the Pacific, where Carroll was a player and then a young assistant in the 1970s. Intrigued by the relatively new field of sports psychol-ogy, he studied everything from the writings of Abraham Maslow to Tim Gallwey's *The Inner Game of Tennis*, becoming convinced that a confident, relaxed athlete was most likely to perform at peak levels. Placed in charge of the secondary, he gathered his defensive backs and asked them which coverages felt most comfortable, which techniques they needed to practice more. An older colleague pulled him aside and said: "Don't you ever ask them what they want; you tell them what they need."

Carroll remained undeterred.

Coaching eventually took him from Ohio State to North Carolina State and then to the NFL, where he became known as a defensive *wunderkind*. But just when his career reached an apex, the New York Jets promoting him to head coach in 1994, troubles arose. The Jets fired him after one year, and he lasted only three seasons as coach of the New England Patriots. The media dismissed him as too quirky, "a transferred surfer from the West Coast who can't handle the pressure of coaching in the East," one columnist wrote. By 2000, Carroll was out of football and considering his options. "They don't understand how hard we work, how we use a different approach to get the same result," he said, adding: "I was angry and frustrated more than anything else."

A year away from the game not only helped to refine his coaching style, it also reinforced his beliefs.

Pete Carroll was a controversial choice as USC's new head coach before the 2001 season.

A Tough Sell

Years later, after all the bowl games and national titles, it is easy to forget about Pete Carroll's tumultuous arrival at USC. The Trojans had courted bigger names such as Dennis Erickson and Mike Bellotti, so Carroll seemed like an afterthought at the time. As word spread that he might be hired, fans reportedly bombarded the athletic department with angry calls and e-mails. This situation was not new to Carroll; critics thought he lacked the experience to coach the New York Jets and the toughness to replace Bill Parcells with the New England Patriots. "I've been an unpopular choice in the past," he said. "What it is, it's a challenge."

At Carroll's first news conference, athletic director Mike Garrett fired back at the doubters, saying, "Joe Blow doesn't know football." A public relations firm provided spin control and Garrett's top assistant, Daryl Gross, told reporters: "I feel like that guy who says, 'Come see it, and if you don't like it, I'll give you your money back.'"

From the start, athletic director Mike Garrett told skeptics that Pete Carroll would become a winner for the Trojans.

So, when USC dumped Paul Hackett at the end of 2000, Carroll went after the job. He was not the Trojans' first choice, nor did everyone agree when athletic director Mike Garrett insisted he had found the right man to restore the

Trojan football legacy. "I saw someone who was a teacher and knew his craft," Garrett said. Carroll immediately announced his intention to win with defense, which sounded like heresy in the high-scoring Pacific-10 Conference. His first season at USC, he also chose to double as defensive coordinator because it gave him an opportunity to work face-to-face with players and ensure that his practices, while energetic and even fun, would be intensely competitive. In time, the program—if not all of college football—realized the new guy was something special. As Nebraska coach Bo Pelini said: "There aren't too many Pete Carrolls out there."

Pete Carroll gets a victor's bath at the 2007 Rose Bowl. Big wins soon proved that USC had hired the right coach.

The Turning Point

Call it instinct. Or experience. Maybe even karma. Something told Kris Richard that the ball was coming his way. The USC cornerback jumped a short route, made the interception, and sailed 58 yards for a touchdown. That quickly, he helped turn around a season and perhaps an entire football program.

Things had not gone well for the Trojans in Pete Carroll's first year as coach in 2001. After rolling over San Jose State in the opener, they went weeks without another victory, playing well enough to stay close but making the same mistakes that had plagued the previous year's team under Paul Hackett. A rout of Arizona State temporarily stopped the bleeding, but USC bungled another game at Notre Dame the following Saturday. Heading into Arizona, the team's record stood at 2–5 and the seniors could see a bowl game slipping away. "I can't worry about that," defensive end Lonnie Ford said.

The Trojans raced to a 31–13 halftime lead in the desert, but they appeared to be headed for another loss when Arizona scrambled back to tie the score at 34–34 in the fourth quarter. USC needed a big play to turn the momen-

Cornerback Kevin Arbet hits a UCLA receiver as the Trojans finish the 2001 regular season with four straight victories and a bowl bid.

tum, and Richard answered with the interception and a winning touchdown in the final two minutes. Carroll sensed something important had transpired, something more than just a victory. Maybe now his players could believe in themselves.

Over the next two weeks, USC slipped past Oregon State in OT and crushed California. Then came 20th-ranked UCLA in the regular-season finale. The Bruins were favored but had suffered from controversy; their star tailback had been suspended for a rules violation. Carson Palmer staked the Trojans to a 7–0 lead, after which the defense hit UCLA with a dizzying array of stunts and blitzes. Cornerback Antuan Simmons made an unlikely interception, trapping a deflected pass against his thigh and bringing it up between his legs, then strutting into the end zone. USC was on the way to a 27–0 win.

A 6–5 record was just good enough to send the Trojans to the Las Vegas Bowl, where they came out flat on Christmas Day, falling to Utah 10–6. Despite a bleak finish, the struggling football program had learned an important lesson. As Carroll told his players in the locker room after the Arizona win: "We don't have to lose anymore."

Reason to Hope

Even as the Trojans struggled through a four-game losing streak early in the 2001 season, there were hints that Pete Carroll had them moving in the right direction. At Oregon, they played a wild game marked by a brawl between the teams before kickoff. USC took a fourth-quarter lead before the seventh-ranked Ducks pulled out a victory on a 32-yard field goal with 12 seconds left. "You think the game is over," quarterback Carson Palmer mused. "You think you've got it won."

Two weeks later, USC lost another heartbreaker to No. 11 Washington, which kicked still another 32-yard field goal with no time remaining. This time, the Trojans could take solace in the fact that they ran the ball effectively, allowing Palmer to be choosy with his passes. Carroll said: "We got so much better today."

The Golden Boy

From the very start, USC fans looked to Carson Palmer as a knight in shining armor, the strong-armed "Golden Boy" who could lead their once-proud team back to prominence. And by the time he was finished with college football, his résumé included an impressive three bowl games and a Heisman Trophy. But the journey was neither easy nor smooth.

Bursting onto the scene in 1998, Palmer came off the bench in his first game as a freshman and with his second pass in the game he completed a 42-yard bomb. He won the starting role by the ninth game of the season, leading the Trojans to a string of victories. Even an upset loss to Texas Christian in the Sun Bowl—the defense sacked him six times—could not dampen expectations.

Then, a few weeks into the 1999 season, Palmer broke his collarbone at Oregon. "Football is my life," he said. "It's what I do every day. It was taken away in one little hit." The tough times were just beginning. The quarterback who returned in 2000 looked as if he were trying too hard, scrambling behind a shaky offensive line, tying a school record with 18 interceptions. His coach, Paul Hackett, was fired and the

Carson Palmer arrived at USC with the size and strength required to be a top college quarterback.

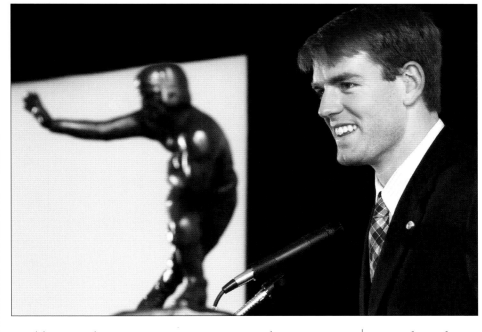

"Golden Boy" hype gave way to suggestions that USC should find another quarterback. The following season, under Pete Carroll and new offensive coordinator Norm Chow, Palmer improved only slightly as the Trojans limped home to a 6–6 record.

But the coaches stuck with him. "It was not his fault. It was just the way we were playing," Chow said. And their patience paid off. As a senior, Palmer grew comfortable with the offense and got some help from a big, talented freshman receiver named Mike Williams. Not only did Palmer win the Heisman by passing for 3,942 yards and 33 touchdowns, including a stellar performance against Notre Dame, he also put USC back in the national spotlight with a victory in the Orange Bowl.

For Palmer, the path to stardom was neither quick nor smooth, winding through injury and rocky stretches. Finally, in 2002, he put together a stellar season, becoming the fifth player in school history to capture the Heisman Trophy.

One Step Closer

All sorts of questions faced USC at the start of 2002. Was this the team that appeared to turn a corner with four consecutive wins the previous season? Or the one that fell flat against Utah in the Las Vegas Bowl? And could quarterback Carson Palmer finally make good on his "Golden Boy" image?

The Trojans block a field-goal try by Iowa in the first half of the 2003 Orange Bowl. USC's 38–16 win pushed them back into the national spotlight.

The early season offered no clear answers. Palmer led his team past Auburn in the opener, sneaking into the end zone with less than two minutes remaining, but the Trojans came up short at Kansas State and blew a game they should have won at Washington State. With their record at 3–2, coach Pete Carroll said: "We have to take care of business. Our hands are full in all phases of the game, and we are really going to have to work our butts off." Facing a pivotal matchup against California, they would require some outside help.

USC fell behind early and was trying to close the gap before halftime when Palmer threw into the end zone, his low pass clearly skipping off the ground before landing in receiver Kareem Kelly's arms. The back judge signaled touchdown. Officials immediately gathered for a conference, but with no instant replay in those days, the call stood and the Trojans were on their way to a 30–28 comeback victory.

The winning continued through October and November, with the team gaining confidence each week. UCLA and Notre Dame fell by the wayside—Palmer secured the Heisman Trophy with four touchdown passes against the Irish—and USC accepted an invitation to play in the Orange Bowl against a powerful Big Ten team from Iowa. "The big old offensive line that we have…we're not going to stretch plays off tackle," Hawkeye running back Fred Russell said. "I think we're just going to run right at them."

Iowa started fast, returning the opening kickoff for a touchdown, but the Hawkeyes underestimated USC's defense, which held Russell and his quarterback, Brad Banks, in check all night. On the other side of the ball, Palmer threw for 303 yards and tailback Justin Fargas busted the game open with a 50-yard touchdown run in the second half. A 38–17 victory lifted USC to No. 4 in the polls, their first Top 10 finish in more than a decade. As the senior Palmer said: "I can't imagine going out any bigger than this."

The Trojans Are Back on Top

The first pass looked easy. Five yards. A touchdown. Just like that, Matt Leinart made his debut as the USC quarterback, guiding his team to a first-quarter lead in the sweltering heat at Auburn. With an aggressive defense to back him up, Leinart played conservatively the rest of the day, picking his spots on the way to a 23–0 win in the 2003 opener. "Like a poised upperclassman and a veteran guy," coach Pete Carroll said. "We were thrilled."

Coming off an Orange Bowl victory the previous season, the Trojans were hungry to keep winning and needed the sophomore Leinart to mature quickly. But one game did not a veteran make, and inexperience caught up with him in a triple-overtime loss at California. The team's title hopes suddenly hung in the balance, as did his starting job, heading into a showdown against Arizona State.

The Sun Devils hit Leinart with a linebacker blitz in the second quarter, sending him to the sideline. When halftime X-rays came back negative, assistant coach Steve Sarkisian told him: "Get back in there." The quarterback hobbled onto the field and completed a pair of clutch passes, the team catching fire for a 37–17 win. "He could have packed his bags and got changed," offensive guard Fred Matua told the *Los Angeles Times*. "He knew we needed him."

> ## "He [Leinart] could have packed his bags and got changed.... He knew we needed him."
>
> ### Fred Matua

The Trojans never looked back, racing through a series of lopsided victories. Linebacker Lofa Tatupu led the defense. Mike Williams dominated at receiver, and freshmen tailbacks Reggie Bush and LenDale White made their "Thunder and Lightning" debut. USC finished the regular season at No. 1 in the AP and *USA Today* polls, but there was a problem—the Bowl Championship Series.

The computer portion of the BCS standings put two other teams in the title game, leaving USC to play Michigan in the Rose Bowl. "If we win that football game, we feel like we'll be the No. 1 team in the country," Carroll said. The Trojans blew past the Wolverines in a contest not nearly as close as the 28–14 score. While Louisiana State captured the BCS crown, USC remained atop the AP Poll, grabbing a share of its first national title since 1978.

LenDale White stretches for a score against Michigan in the 2004 Rose Bowl. USC won to earn a share of the national title.

The Ugly Duckling Grows Up

Back in grade school, he was chubby and cross-eyed, forced to wear Coke-bottle glasses. Sometimes the other kids teased him. Matt Leinart still had a long way to go on the road to football stardom.

The journey began with a growth spurt that made him tall and lean, and surgery followed to correct his eyes. As for the sports part, his older brother lent a helping hand. Ryan Leinart, a baseball and basketball player in high school, had always regretted not trying football, so he paid for his little brother to attend a local camp where the coaches saw potential.

There would be more challenges. After his freshman year at Mater Dei

Matt Leinart continued the modern tradition of USC quarterbacks.

High School, Leinart needed shoulder surgery. Two strong seasons earned him a scholarship to USC, but he had to wait on the sideline while Carson Palmer won a Heisman Trophy. And when Palmer graduated, there was a three-way fight for the starting job, with Leinart barely winning out over Brandon Hance and Matt Cassel, who later played for the New England Patriots.

Leinart's arm wasn't particularly strong nor was he blazingly fast, but he more than compensated with coolness under pressure and an uncanny sense for reading defenses, changing plays at the line of scrimmage. "He knows where to go with the football," Oregon State coach Mike Riley said. "He handles all parts of being a quarterback." This instinct translated into almost 7,000 yards passing, two national titles, and a Heisman of his own after two seasons as the starter. Then Leinart cemented his legacy at USC by postponing NFL dollars to return as a senior. "He wants to play with his teammates," coach Pete Carroll said. "There was no amount of money that could take that away from him, and I think that's an extraordinary statement."

The 2005 season was perfect with 12 consecutive wins until a loss to Texas in the BCS national championship game. For his USC career, Leinart amassed a 37–2 record, with 10,693 yards and 99 touchdowns through the air, placing him second on the school's all-time passing list behind Palmer. Leinart said: "We're just a bunch of kids going out there and playing football. There's nothing better than that."

Leinart's quarterback sneak, which led the Trojans to a win over Notre Dame in 2005, is trumpeted in the Los Angeles Times.

"It Doesn't Get Any Sweeter"

The Trojans had reasons for coming out flat in their 2004 season opener. They took the field without star receiver Mike Williams, who tried to turn professional and lost college eligibility. They played in a suburb of Washington, D.C., where most fans at FedEx Field rooted against them. And they faced a talented Virginia Tech team.

Two things happened to save the day. The offense found a replacement for Williams, turning to explosive tailback Reggie Bush, whose three long touchdown catches gave the Trojans a lead. Then the defense clamped down to preserve a 24–13 victory.

A Heisman Showdown

The 2005 national championship game made college football history: It marked the first time that Heisman Trophy winners faced each other. USC quarterback Matt Leinart (right) had collected the trophy a month earlier. Oklahoma's Jason White had won the previous season, but his team lost in the 2004 title game, so he was returning to settle a score.

"The biggest thing that sticks in my head was the e-mails I got last year... saying that I need to give back the Heisman Trophy," White said. "Stuff like that motivates me."

His second chance did not turn out much better. Though White completed more than 66 percent of his passes against USC, he also suffered three interceptions in a 55–19 loss. Leinart, meanwhile, had an MVP performance with 332 yards passing and a bowl-record five touchdowns.

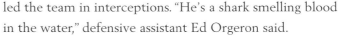

With Carroll's background as an NFL coordinator, it made sense that his best team to date excelled at stopping opponents cold. Defensive linemen Shaun Cody and Mike Patterson dominated in the trenches, allowing middle linebacker Lofa Tatupu to make plays at the point of attack. Darnell Bing anchored the secondary, and undersized linebacker Matt Grootegoed led the team in interceptions. "He's a shark smelling blood in the water," defensive assistant Ed Orgeron said.

There were close calls along the way. USC needed some halftime group therapy to come back at Stanford and a goal-line push in the final minutes against California. Bush provided more heroics by way of a zigzagging punt return to defeat Oregon State on a cold, foggy night in Corvallis. After rolling over Notre Dame and defeating UCLA, the Trojans were headed to face Oklahoma for the national championship at the Orange Bowl.

The title game turned into a coronation, with USC blowing past the Sooners. Matt Leinart was masterful with five touchdown passes and LenDale White pounded for 118 yards. The defense all but shut down Oklahoma running back Adrian Peterson, holding him to 82 yards. It all added up to a 55–19 victory and an undisputed title. "This was as close to perfect as you can get," tight end Dominique Byrd said. "It doesn't get any sweeter."

Lofa Tatupu celebrates a sack against Oklahoma in the 2005 Orange Bowl. Defense played a crucial role in the Trojans' perfect season.

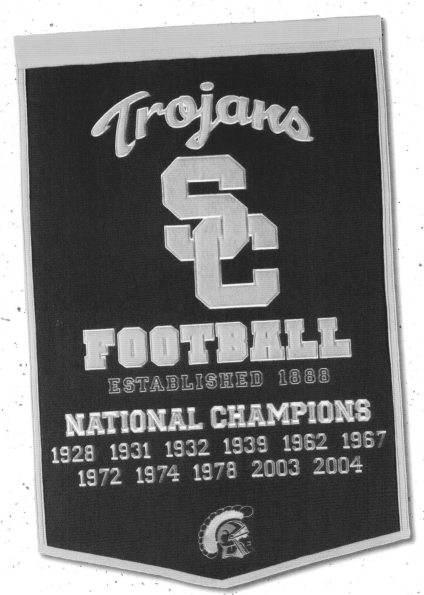

With 11 national championships, USC ranks among the most successful programs in the history of college football. Trojan fans proudly hang this banner.

Tailback Reggie Bush made big news in December 2005, adding his name to the list of six previous Trojans who had captured the coveted Heisman Trophy.

Los Angeles Times
SPORTS

Sunday, December 11, 2005   latimes.com/sports

Clippers Keep Party Going

L.A. is fueled by home crowd and puts an end to Phoenix's nine-game winning streak, 101-91.

By Jason Reid
Times Staff Writer

There's a hot party happening at Staples Center and everyone is welcome, though the hosts have been rude to some.

Opposing teams haven't had much fun during a Clipper bash that raged on Saturday night in a 101-91 victory over the Phoenix Suns.

The Clippers rocked off the game's hottest team in a showdown for first place in the Pacific Division, ending the Suns' NBA-best winning streak at nine games while improving to 9-1 at Staples Center in their second consecutive game without injured forward Corey Maggette.

Forward Elton Brand scored 27 points and grabbed 13 rebounds for his 13th double-double, and Cuttino Mobley scored 25, point guard Sam Cassell had 24 and center Chris Kaman contributed 12 points and 10 rebounds as the Clippers took charge with defense in the second half to go 3-6 on a four-game road trip.

(See Clippers, Page D7)

Jackson in Foul Mood

Laker win streak ends against Timberwolves, 95-82, and the coach complains about calls.

By Mike Brennahan
Times Staff Writer

MINNEAPOLIS — The Lakers pleaded and pleaded but couldn't take the fifth.

Faced with a perceived injustice in free-throw shooting, as a game slipped away, they unraveled as a game slipped away, the Lakers fell to the Minnesota Timberwolves, 95-82, and attempt to win five consecutive games ended up well short Saturday at Target Center.

Trying to win five in a row for the first time since April 2004, the Lakers returned to a familiar, old pattern of not passing enough and threw in a twist by complaining about the referees.

Laker Coach Phil Jackson seemed particularly annoyed during the game, repeatedly asking.

(See Lakers, Page D7)

REGGIE BUSH WINS USC'S SEVENTH HEISMAN TROPHY

1965	1968	1979	1981	2002	2004	2005
MIKE GARRETT Tailback, 1963-65	O.J. SIMPSON Tailback, 1967-68	CHARLES WHITE Tailback, 1976-79	MARCUS ALLEN Tailback, 1978-81	CARSON PALMER Quarterback, 1998-02	MATT LEINART Quarterback, 2002-05	REGGIE BUSH Tailback, 2003-05

He's No Mere Poser

Bush is the best player of 2005, and some are calling him one of best college tailbacks ever

By David Wharton
Times Staff Writer

As Reggie Bush stood before a national television audience and accepted the Heisman Trophy on Saturday night, at least one question was settled.

The best player in college football this season? The answer — officially — was Bush. The USC tailback won over teammate Matt Leinart and Texas quarterback Vince Young by a landslide.

But the lineup of previous winners standing behind him on stage in New York, a who's who that ranged from Tony Dorsett to Billy Sims to Eddie George, begged another question.

Where does Bush rate historically?

People in and around the game, having already sent a good number of superlatives his direction this fall, used different measuring sticks.

Terry Bowden, the former coach and current television analyst, places Bush in the rarified company of Barry Sanders and Michael Vick.

"One of the best I've ever seen," Bowden said. "You put him on a field with other athletes and he makes them look

(See Bush, Page D8)

BILL PLASCHKE

Bush and Leinart Push Each Other Into Greatness

NEW YORK — Reggie Bush won, but it was Matt Leinart who pumped his left fist.

Reggie Bush won, but it was Matt Leinart who reached out for the first hug.

The USC running back won, but, as his lingering embrace with the USC quarterback illustrated, we all won, witnessing young men who did not personify the word "Heisman" as much as they defined the word "teammate."

Reggie Bush, who accepted the Heisman Trophy as the best player in college football Saturday, nearly wept while delivering his acceptance speech.

Matt Leinart, who won the award last year, nearly wept when that speech included his name.

Bush thanked Leinart for changing his life.

(See Plaschke, Page D10)

HERITAGE HAUL: USC tailback Reggie Bush received the largest percentage of first-place votes in Heisman Trophy history (784 of 892, 87.9%) in becoming the Trojans' third Heisman winner in the last four years.

Sweeping the nation

Regional points breakdown of the finalists in balloting for the 2005 Heisman Trophy.

NORTHEAST		MID-ATLANTIC		SOUTH		SOUTHWEST		MIDWEST		FAR WEST	
1. Reggie Bush	432	1. Reggie Bush	416	1. Reggie Bush	416	1. Reggie Bush	436	1. Reggie Bush	439	1. Reggie Bush	432
2. Vince Young	262	2. Vince Young	256	2. Vince Young	273	2. Vince Young	302	2. Vince Young	291	2. Vince Young	230
3. Matt Leinart	133	3. Matt Leinart	177	3. Matt Leinart	135	3. Matt Leinart	112	3. Matt Leinart	122	3. Matt Leinart	150
4. Brady Quinn	53	4. Brady Quinn	29	4. Brady Quinn	37	4. Brady Quinn	19	4. Brady Quinn	30	4. Brady Quinn	21

Source: Associated Press

RELATED STORY

Bush landslide: Running back becomes seventh Trojan to win the Heisman. A1

This miniature version of Tommy Trojan includes the same plumed helmet, shield, and sword as the full-size statue that stands at the center of campus.

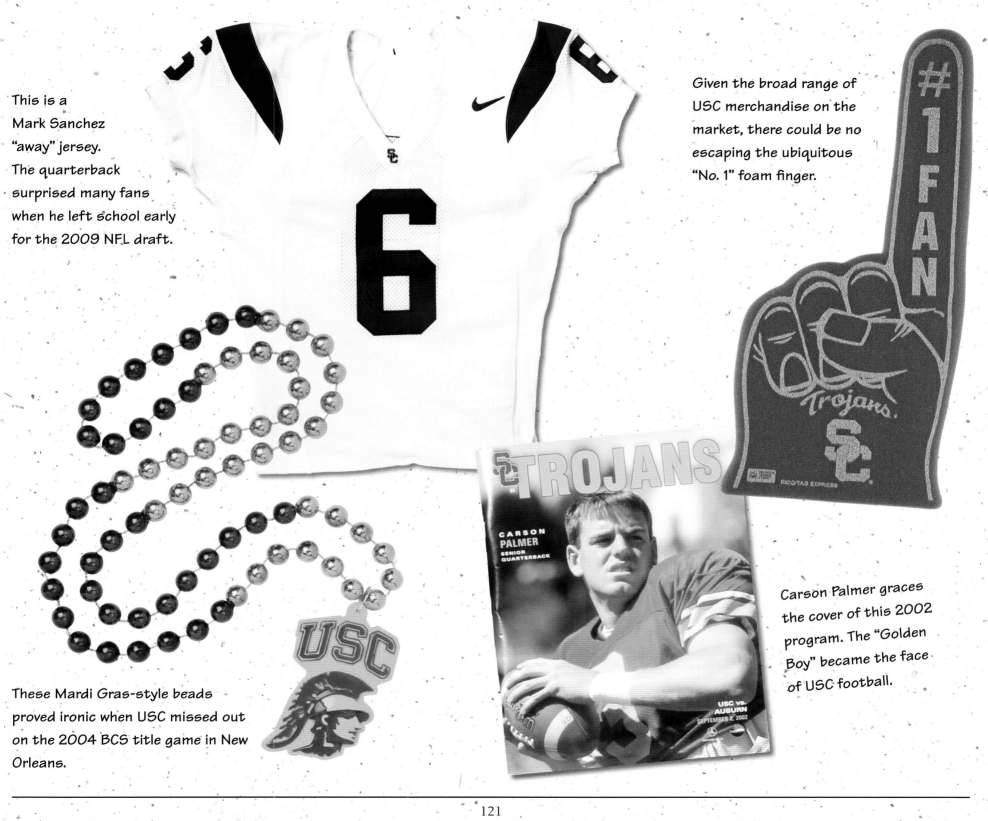

This is a Mark Sanchez "away" jersey. The quarterback surprised many fans when he left school early for the 2009 NFL draft.

Given the broad range of USC merchandise on the market, there could be no escaping the ubiquitous "No. 1" foam finger.

These Mardi Gras-style beads proved ironic when USC missed out on the 2004 BCS title game in New Orleans.

CARSON PALMER
SENIOR QUARTERBACK

USC vs. AUBURN
SEPTEMBER 2, 2002

Carson Palmer graces the cover of this 2002 program. The "Golden Boy" became the face of USC football.

The Bush Push

The clock was ticking toward zero as Matt Leinart hustled his offense to the line; they were down by three points, a yard short of the end zone. With no time-outs, the USC coaches signaled that he had the option to spike the ball and bring out the field-goal unit. Many in sold-out Notre Dame Stadium figured the game was headed for OT.

No matter what happened in the final seconds, the 2005 USC–Notre Dame rivalry already qualified as a classic. The Trojans, favored to win their third consecutive national championship, were halfway through an undefeated season and ranked No. 1. The Irish were back in the national spotlight under first-year coach Charlie Weis.

Quarterback Matt Leinart got credit for this last-second touchdown to defeat Notre Dame in 2005, but tailback Reggie Bush (5) deserves an assist for the push that helped propel Leinart across the goal line.

Starting at their 25-yard line, the Trojans soon faced fourth and nine. Amid the roar of an enemy stadium, Leinart called an audible and looked toward receiver Dwayne Jarrett down the sideline. "I actually thought I underthrew the ball," he said. The pass was just good enough, and Jarrett made a clutch catch and sprinted 61 yards deep into Irish territory.

A few plays later, a scrambling Leinart got hit short of the end zone and fumbled out of bounds. The clock ran down to 0:00, but officials correctly ruled that it should have stopped at seven seconds.

One play remained, and Leinart knew he had an option to run. Bush told him to go for it, then he saw the Notre Dame defense bunched at the line of scrimmage and yelled, "No, no, no." It was too late. Leinart took the snap and hit a wall of bodies, spinning to his left, extending the ball over his head. Bush ran up from behind to give him a shove, nudging him over the goal line. It was an illegal maneuver, but no flags were thrown and USC won 34–31. As Weis later said, "That's heads-up by Reggie. And hopefully any running back I had would be pushing."

No lead was safe on a day when offense prevailed. Reggie Bush scored three times, highlighted by a 36-yard run in which he hurdled a defender at full speed. Notre Dame answered with quarterback Brady Quinn scrambling and passing at will. His five-yard touchdown run gave the Irish a 31–28 lead with 2:04 remaining, leaving USC just enough time for a last-ditch effort.

"A Little Juke, and He's Gone"

It took just one practice—and two words—for Pete Carroll to define his newest tailback. The USC coach watched Reggie Bush at the start of the 2003 training camp and said the freshman possessed extraordinary "speed" and "wiggle."

Reggie Bush leaps over a UCLA defender in the 2005 crosstown rivalry game. Spectacular runs such as this made Bush one of the most exciting players in college football history.

As a boy growing up in San Diego, Bush played tag for hours, dodging, spinning, and eluding friends. His parents looked for ways to exhaust his boundless energy, enrolling him in karate and youth baseball, until he finally asked to play football. From his very first Pop Warner game—onlookers swear he ran for about 300 yards—Bush showed glimpses of the talent that would make him a prep All-American and a star by his sophomore year in college. "I was playing a game I loved," he said. "A game I was supposed to play."

No other player was more responsible for USC's 2004 national championship. Three touchdowns in a close win against Virginia Tech. A critical 65-yard punt return at Oregon State. Two long scoring runs at UCLA. "Even if you think you have him, he can give you a little juke and he's gone," Washington State linebacker Pat Bennett said. Or, as Virginia Tech coach Frank Beamer put it: "He can turn a game around in a hurry."

By 2005, the Trojans had learned to use Bush at tailback, split wide, anything to get the ball in his hands. His 1,740 rushing yards included dazzling runs against Washington and Fresno State, and he also had the timely assist at Notre Dame, shoving quarterback Matt Leinart into the end zone for the winning touchdown.

Leaving school after his junior season, Bush slipped in the NFL Draft and came under NCAA investigation for allegedly accepting cash from agents while in school. But his exploits on the field—along with the 2005 Heisman Trophy—rank him among USC's greatest tailbacks.

Thunder and Lightning

Reggie Bush wasn't the only star tailback during his three seasons at USC. In terms of career rushing yards, he was only slightly better than another runner with whom he shared the ball. LenDale White joined the team out of Colorado at the same time as Bush. In their third game as freshmen, against Hawaii, they combined for 112 yards and 4 touchdowns, earning the nickname "Thunder and Lightning" because of their contrasting styles. While Bush had videogame speed, White used his 235-pound frame to bull through the line. He actually out-rushed Bush in their first two seasons before they each surpassed 1,000 yards as juniors.

White ran for more than 100 yards against ASU in 2005.

"When you have a big back that pounds the ball and then a guy like Reggie Bush who's shifty, that's a big change," Texas defensive lineman Rod Wright said. "It's hard to play both of them."

Taking a Run at History

Dwayne Jarrett crosses the goal line against Texas, but the Trojans came up short in the 2006 national title game, losing their shot at a third straight championship.

Nineteen seconds stood between USC and college football history. If the top-ranked Trojans could hang on for 26 more seconds, they would defeat second-ranked Texas in the Rose Bowl for an unprecedented third consecutive national championship. All they had to do was stop the Longhorns' lethal quarterback, Vince Young, from crossing the goal line.

Coming into the 2005 title game, USC owned a 34-game winning streak despite a shaky defense that was uncharacteristic of coach Carroll's program. The Trojans had survived close calls against Notre Dame and Fresno State by putting up big numbers with the Heisman duo of Matt Leinart and Reggie Bush. As Texas coach Mack Brown said: "'SC is going to make plays." But the Longhorns had Young, a dual threat out of the backfield who had something to prove after finishing second to Bush in the Heisman voting.

In Pasadena, USC scored quickly, then squandered several opportunities. Texas eventually found a rhythm, taking a 16–10 lead into halftime. Bush later mused: "We tried to do too much."

Neither team flinched in a raucous second half. LenDale White scored twice in the third quarter and a Leinart to Dwayne Jarrett pass in the fourth gave USC a 12-point lead in the fourth quarter. With just over four minutes remaining, Young reversed field and swept right for a 17-yard touchdown, closing the gap to 38–33.

The Trojans got the ball back and had a chance to secure victory. On fourth and two near midfield, the Texas defense stopped White short of a first down. "In my way of thinking," Carroll said, "you go for it all the time." Texas quickly mounted a drive, Young scrambled and threw, setting up a fourth-down play at the 8-yard line with those 26 seconds remaining. Lined up in a shotgun formation, the lanky quarterback looked briefly to pass before taking off, out-racing two defenders to the end zone. Texas had a 41–38 win, and USC had been denied a victory for the ages. "It's been wonderful," Carroll said of his team's winning streak. "Too bad it had to end."

The Fruits of Victory

Though the Trojans failed to win a record third consecutive national championship in 2005, they made history in other ways.

Trailing at Arizona State in the fourth game, USC scored 21 unanswered points to rack up a Pac-10 Conference–record 26th consecutive victory. The "Bush Push" at Notre Dame helped set a new school record with 13 straight wins on the road. After defeating UCLA in the regular-season finale, the Trojans walked away with a Pac-10 record 27 consecutive victories at home and an NCAA record for defeating 16 AP ranked teams in a row.

A New Team on the Field

John David Booty took over at quarterback in 2006, guiding the Trojans to another Rose Bowl.

Heisman Trophy winners Matt Leinart and Reggie Bush were gone to the NFL. So were much of the offensive line and a good chunk of the defense. It is hard to imagine any team facing the changes that confronted the Trojans in 2006, yet the major polls ranked them in the Top 10 to start the season.

This optimism centered on quarterback John David Booty, who had waited patiently behind Leinart for his chance. The quiet Louisiana native looked to get help from veteran receivers Dwayne Jarrett and Steve Smith and a defense bolstered by talented underclassmen. Arkansas was first on the schedule, and Razorback coach Houston Nutt said: "There is a reason why [USC] is ranked No. 6 in the country."

The Trojans started with wins over the Razorbacks and Nebraska. Though the offense lacked killer instinct and the defense had yet to reach top form, hopes continued to run high for another title run. Even after a loss at Oregon State—the Beavers swatted away Booty's pass on a two-point attempt to tie the game in the final seconds—coach Pete Carroll remained characteristically positive. "I don't want to lower our standards and expectations," he said.

His team rebounded with three wins over ranked opponents, but any chance at the Bowl Championship Series title finally perished at UCLA. Booty had yet another fourth-quarter pass tipped near the line—this one was intercepted—as the underdog Bruins scored a shocking 13–9 upset.

USC accepted an invitation to the Rose Bowl with Booty vowing: "We don't want to go into the offseason with that bitter taste in our mouths." On New Year's Day, the Trojans played Big Ten rival Michigan to a 3–3 tie in the first half, then they showed the offensive spark that had been lacking for much of the season. Booty passed for 391 yards and 4 touchdowns to lead the Trojans to a 32–18 win.

Talent Grab

Quiet and shy off the field, Troy Polamalu ranks among the toughest players in USC history.

With three Heisman Trophy winners in four years (from 2002 to 2005), it was no surprise that the offense grabbed much of the spotlight at USC. Start with a front line that featured Jacob Rogers, Taitusi Lutui, and three-time All-American Sam Baker at left tackle. Add a string of gifted receivers in Mike Williams, Dwayne Jarrett, Steve Smith, and tight end Fred Davis. Jarrett credited his leaping, juggling touchdowns to boyhood afternoons in New Jersey, practicing in the backyard with an uncle who "forced me to make one-hand catches."

The talent level at USC rose dramatically under Pete Carroll because the former NFL coach took to recruiting with a fervor that verged on maniacal. He started by visiting scores of high school coaches throughout Southern California, determined to keep local prospects at home. Then he went after some of the best players nationwide, attracting blue-chip recruits from Florida, New Jersey, and Colorado. It wasn't just the offense that benefited. Carroll, after all, had made his reputation as a defensive coordinator, so he wanted to build a tough, aggressive defense. And he set the tone with a young safety named Troy Polamalu.

With a demeanor that verged on monklike, Polamalu arrived at USC as an unheralded prospect from a small town in Oregon, invited mainly because his uncle, Kennedy Pola, was the Trojans' running backs coach. Polamalu would say a brief prayer before each snap, explaining that "you don't want to go out there and break a guy's neck." But as a teammate pointed out, Polamalu could seem "real quiet... and then he turns into a beast." Not only did he lead the team in tackles his junior year in 2001, but his dramatic flair translated into game-changing interceptions and blocked punts.

The Trojans continued to gather All-Americans on defense. Shaun Cody, Mike Patterson, and big Kenechi Udeze terrorized opponents along the line of scrimmage. Lofa Tatupu, Keith Rivers, and Rey Maualuga—who ranked among the most physically talented athletes in school history—forged a new tradition for USC linebackers. The secondary featured stars such as Darnell Bing and Taylor Mays. "The difference is Pete," the legendary San Francisco 49ers coach Bill Walsh once said. "He hasn't rested on his laurels."

> **"The difference is Pete [Carroll]. He hasn't rested on his laurels."**
>
> **Bill Walsh**

Three Who Were Lost

Mario Danelo was a record-setting kicker for USC before dying in an offseason accident.

When USC scored its first touchdown of the 2007 season, there was something odd about the extra-point team that ran onto the field: no kicker. The Trojans were paying tribute to Mario Danelo, their record-setting kicker who had died in the offseason, falling from an ocean cliff near his home in San Pedro. They waited in missing-man formation until the clock expired and officials penalized them for delay of game. Then the new kicker, David Buehler, came off the sideline for the conversion.

Memorials were becoming all too common at USC. The team suffered a major off-the-field loss when longtime assistant Marv Goux died of cancer in the summer of 2002. Though Goux had retired years before, the fiery coach remained a strong presence, often summoned to give pep talks before big games. The university honored him with a memorial service beside Tommy Trojan—the band playing some of his favorite songs—and players spent the following season wearing a football-shaped sticker with his name on their helmets.

The next summer brought more sad news with the death of Drean Rucker. A blue-chip recruit from nearby Moreno Valley, Rucker was two weeks from starting his first training camp when he went to the beach with friends and drowned in a rip current. Though not yet an official member of the team, the young linebacker had spent much of his vacation working out

USC honored Danelo before the opening game of the 2007 season. It would have been his senior season.

with USC players. During the 2003 season, defensive end Kenechi Udeze dedicated the first tackle of each game to Rucker's memory, and coach Pete Carroll announced that no one would wear his jersey number 54. "Drean was a wonderful young man with a great spirit," Carroll said. "He would light up a room with his smile."

Danelo was part of the same freshman class, arriving as a walk-on and earning a scholarship two seasons later. The son of former NFL kicker Joe Danelo, Mario set an NCAA record for extra points attempted and made during the high-scoring 2005 season. His two field goals helped USC to the victory over Michigan in the 2007 Rose Bowl. A week later, Danelo was found dead. "He was big-time about living life and having fun," Carroll said. "He lived it hard and fun and fast—he enjoyed it."

The Defense Makes a Stand

The path that led USC to the 2008 Rose Bowl felt more like a roller-coaster ride. After spending the first month of the 2007 season at No. 1, the Trojans suffered one of the biggest upsets in college football history, falling to 41-point underdog Stanford at the Coliseum. Then quarterback John David Booty sat out with a broken finger and they lost again three weeks later, this time on the road at Oregon. Finally, with the season threatening to unravel, the team rebounded for a series of victories to salvage a tie for the Pac-10 title. "Every chance we get, we want to win this thing," coach Pete Carroll said of the conference race. "And get ourselves in that Rose Bowl."

They earned the right to face Illinois, a Big Ten team that brought a potent ground game to complement solid defense. The Illini also had a wild card in Juice Williams, the type of running quarterback who had given USC fits in the past.

But come New Year's Day, the USC defense never gave Williams a chance to get untracked. The offense scored quickly with Booty—now healed—throwing the first touchdown pass, and reserve quarterback Garrett Green adding another on a trick play. The best that Illinois could manage was a field goal as the Trojans stretched their lead to 21–3 by halftime. The Illini had one more chance to make a game of it, scoring early in the third quarter, which led to a critical play.

With the Illini threatening to score again, USC linebacker Kaluka Maiava punched the ball out of receiver Jacob Willis's hands short of the goal line. USC pounced on the fumble. As

Illinois linebacker J. Leman said, things "just kind of went downhill from there." The Illini kept losing the ball, and USC turned their miscues into TDs, which added up to a 49–17 rout. Booty and the rest of the offense generated a Rose Bowl–record 633 total yards, while the defense held Williams to minus 19 yards rushing, recovering two fumbles and intercepting two passes. "I think we've proven something," linebacker Rey Maualuga said. "Tonight just shows what we are and what we're capable of."

Tailback Joe McKnight had 206 all-purpose yards, including a touchdown, against Illinois in the Trojans' 2008 Rose Bowl victory.

A New Standard for Success

Howard Jones won 11 games in a season once. John McKay did it twice. John Robinson did it three times. But when the Trojans defeated Illinois in the 2008 Rose Bowl, Pete Carroll secured his sixth consecutive season of 11 wins or more in only seven years as coach at USC. That streak set a new standard for success. Carroll credited his players.

"A long time ago we talked about 'Win forever,'" he said. "That's kind of what these guys have done. We couldn't be more proud, couldn't be more indebted to their willingness to do the stuff and craziness we've taken them through to show they're this special and unique. They should always be remembered for that."

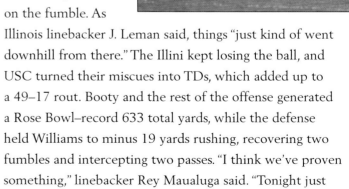

Carroll ranks among USC's top coaches.

Even with a string of Heisman Trophy winners on offense, the Trojans under Pete Carroll have made their mark by stopping opponents.

The Other Side of Winning

USC fans gather at the Coliseum peristyle prior to kickoff. Saturday crowds became larger after Pete Carroll arrived and the Trojans began winning.

The Coliseum was about half-full for Pete Carroll's first game at USC. The new coach talked about putting on "a big show," hoping to get more fans in those sections of empty seats. It didn't take long.

With each winning season, each trip to a major bowl game, the crowds grew larger and larger. Average attendance swelled toward 90,000 in a few years, and people around the nation took notice. "I continue to be amazed by the USC fans," ESPN analyst Kirk Herbstreit wrote. The former Ohio State quarterback was part of the network's *GameDay* show that aired from USC once or twice a season. "Keep in mind we go live at 7 A.M. local time. It's dark out, but the Trojan fan base shows its support for the team. They are changing the national image of Pac-10 fans by themselves."

Halfway through the 2004 season, the Trojans celebrated their 50-millionth fan, and on some Saturdays, it seemed like all of them were trying to get inside the Coliseum at once. Sheer volume forced people to arrive a little earlier, park a little farther away, and work harder to find open spots for their tailgate parties. Scalpers got higher prices for their tickets, and students began lining up outside—their section is first-come, first-served—hours before kickoff. School and stadium officials also had to change their routine.

More than 1,000 people work in and around the Coliseum on Saturdays, a staff that ranges from ticket takers to groundskeepers to electricians. Police walk the grounds while an additional 60 to 100 off-duty officers join with a large force of yellow-jacketed security guards inside. The day begins early because, as stadium general manager Pat Lynch explained, "someone has to get there to cook the hot dogs and make the coffee."

As many as 36,000 cars show up for games, traffic officers guiding them toward parking lots where the prices run as high as $100 for big games. The stadium gates occasionally bottleneck as ushers try to get people to their seats by kickoff. The rush doesn't stop there.

Maintenance workers attend to broken seats during the game. Workers with walkie-talkies coordinate the halftime shows and direct medical personnel to fans who fall ill. And when the clock ticks down to 0:00, there are 90,000 people to get back in their cars and back on the road as yet another crew begins the arduous job of cleaning the stadium for the next weekend.

The Tailback in Charge

The man who stood at the podium looked fit for his age, with a powerful build and the determined glare of an athlete. In many ways, the 48-year-old Mike Garrett still resembled one of the toughest players in USC history. Yet on that January day in 1993 when he was named athletic director at his alma mater, Garrett had to fight back tears. "There has been no prouder moment than this for me," he said. "I came here in 1962, and we have been through a lot—a lot of good, a lot of indifferent. But you know the amazing thing about it, it's still great to be a Trojan."

Garrett had spent a good deal of time away from the university after winning the Heisman Trophy and then graduating in 1967. His NFL career lasted eight years, highlighted by two trips to the Super Bowl and 1,000-yard seasons with the Kansas City Chiefs and San Diego Chargers. Life after football included management positions in business, political campaigns in the early 1980s, then a law degree from Western State University College of Law. In 1990, Garrett was thinking about purchasing a beer distributorship when Mike McGee, then the USC athletic director, called. "He had some issues that needed to be dealt with," Garrett said. "Mike asked me to come back."

Many assumed that when Garrett took the job as associate athletic director, he would eventually succeed McGee. But when McGee announced that he was leaving two years later, there was considerable opposition from alumni who saw Garrett as too serious, demanding, alternately warm and gruff. "People thought there might be a better man for the job," he said. This sentiment lingered

Mike Garrett rejoices in a 2004 national title with Pete Carroll, the man he hired to restore the USC football tradition. As the school's athletic director, Garrett oversaw construction of a sports arena on campus.

for a few years, kept alive by the awkward firing of John Robinson, the failure of Paul Hackett, and finally Pete Carroll's controversial hiring.

But by the fall of 2008, any grumbling had quieted to a faint memory. Under Garrett, USC had won 18 national titles in 10 different sports and boosted its annual athletic budget to $72 million with increased fundraising. Just across the street from campus stood a testament to the former tailback's resolve—after years of false starts, the university finally had a new basketball arena. Most of all, Garrett had fulfilled his primary duty as athletic director. "The whole catch to this place," he explained, "is to win national championships in football."

Among the Game's Elite

The morning after the Trojans defeated Oklahoma for the 2004 national championship, a bleary Pete Carroll stood at the podium to receive the crystal trophy. He and his players had stayed up all night celebrating their second consecutive title—"It was Mardi Gras right there at the Diplomat," he said—and now he faced questions about the "D" word. As in dynasty. The coach wasn't making any predictions about winning the following year, but he told reporters: "We do know how to do it."

Ranking the greatest college football programs of all time can be tricky. There have been numerous split championships, especially in the years before 1936 when rival polls each named their own No. 1 team. By most accepted counts, the Trojans have captured 11 titles, placing them in the rarified company of Alabama, Notre Dame, and Michigan.

The Associated Press poll, the gold standard from 1936 until the creation of the Bowl Championship Series in 1998, confirms USC's standing among the game's elite. At the start of the 2008 season, the Trojans had been included in the AP rankings a total of 651 weeks and had held the top spot for 81 of those weeks, which placed them among the top five schools of all-time. They also owned the record for staying at No. 1 for 33 consecutive weeks from 2003 into 2005.

Pete Carroll holds up the crystal trophy signifying that USC has won the national championship for the 2004 season.

During that span, USC became only the second team to lead the AP wire-to-wire, opening the 2004 season at No. 1 in the preseason polls and finishing with that championship victory over the Sooners. The morning after the 2004 win, Carroll could not see any reason for this success to end. "Our system is in order now," he said. "We know what we're doing, we know how we want to do it."

In the Top 10

A history of USC in the major national polls:

1938: 7 (AP)	1976: 2 (AP), 2 (UPI)
1939: 3 (AP)	1978: 2 (AP), 1 (UPI)
1944: 7 (AP)	1979: 2 (AP), 2 (UPI)
1947: 8 (AP)	1984: 10 (AP), 9 (UPI)
1952: 5 (AP), 4 tie (UPI)	1988: 7 (AP), 9 (UPI), 7 (USA)
1962: 1 (AP), 1 (UPI)	1989: 8 (AP), 9 (UPI), 7 (USA)
1964: 10 (AP), 10 (UPI)	2002: 4 (AP), 4 (USA)
1965: 10 (AP), 9 (UPI)	2003: 1 (AP), 2 (USA)
1967: 1 (AP), 1 (UPI)	2004: 1 (AP), 1 (USA)
1968: 4 (AP), 2 (UPI)	2005: 2 (AP), 2 (USA)
1969: 3 (AP), 4 (UPI)	2006: 4 (AP), 4 (USA)
1972: 1 (AP), 1 (UPI)	2007: 3 (AP), 2 (USA)
1973: 8 (AP), 7 (UPI)	2008: 3 (AP), 2 (USA)
1974: 2 (AP), 1 (UPI)	

The Trojans won three national championships before 1936 and another in 1939, awarded by the Dickinson System. AP is the Associated Press (1936 to present), UPI is United Press International (1950–95), USA is *USA Today* (1982 to present).

Home Sweet Home

The news broke toward the end of the 2007 season. As the Trojans put together a winning streak to earn a share of the conference title, word leaked out that they might abandon their home in the Coliseum. It seemed implausible, if only because the team had played under the peristyle arches for more than 80 years, but the lease was running out and the university was looking elsewhere.

School administrators said they were frustrated because the historic venue had fallen into disrepair since its last facelift more than a decade earlier. Tired of hearing promises, they offered to spend $100 million for upgrades in return for a master lease that gave them authority to operate the stadium. The Coliseum Commission—a mixture of state and local representatives—insisted on retaining its power. The situation quickly deteriorated.

First, USC initiated talks to move to Pasadena and share the Rose Bowl with UCLA. Then, after athletic director Mike Garrett sent an e-mail asking fans to get involved, stadium officials began getting angry calls and death threats. "That's taking it to a low, low level," one commissioner said. The mayor and other civic officials jumped in, urging a settlement. Finally, in the spring of 2008, the two sides reached an agreement.

The 25-year lease gave USC a seat on the Coliseum Commission and veto power over any NFL team returning to the stadium. In exchange, the university allowed the commission to use its name and logo to seek a lucrative naming-rights deal. The contract included an escape clause for USC should the commission fail to make good on a number of promised improvements, but work began immediately and some new features were in place a few months later.

By the start of the 2008 season, crumbling concrete had been patched and a million-dollar sound system pumped music to all parts of the bowl. Fans got new seats in the corners of the east end zone and additional concession stands with an area to watch a big-screen television.

The players were excited about the $2-million high definition video board beside the Olympic torch. Fullback Stanley Havili explained that he often glanced up at the board after big plays. "I want to see what happened," he said.

The 2008 Trojans make their traditional walk down the Coliseum steps before the game.

Right at the Top

Mark Sanchez became the USC quarterback amid great expectations in 2008.

The problem with building a powerhouse football program is that fans and the media expect a championship every season. Even before USC played its first game in the fall of the 2008, Pete Carroll faced questions about the national picture, strength of schedule, and most importantly, where his team might fit into the polls. "It doesn't mean a darn thing to us," he said. "It's a little bit of a popularity contest, you know." The coach had more pressing matters to address.

The season began with a change at quarterback. John David Booty had left for the NFL, replaced by the strong and mobile Mark Sanchez, a fiery leader who could be something of a gambler on the field. Sanchez wasted no time asserting himself, passing for 338 yards and three touchdowns as USC rolled past Virginia 52–7 in the opener. That victory lifted the team to No. 1 and set the stage for a showdown with No. 5 Ohio State at the Coliseum. In what many were calling the game of the year, the Trojans gave up an early field goal and nothing more and Sanchez threw another four touchdown passes in a 35–3 rout. "A day you grow up dreaming about," he called it, lingering on the field afterward. "I just wanted to look at everything and feel everything."

Fans were dreaming too, envisioning another championship trophy. But that big win might have taken something out of the players; they looked flat against Oregon State in the next game, tackling poorly and making key mistakes. Any hopes of slipping past the Beavers ended with Sanchez's late interception, the final blunder in a 27–21 upset loss. That quickly, the season turned upside down.

While much of the attention focused on their quarterback, the Trojans had something else going for them. Rey Maualuga and Brian Cushing, perhaps the best linebacker duo in the country, formed the core of a defense that quickly bounced back from the nightmare in Corvallis. Safeties Taylor Mays and Kevin Ellison anchored the secondary, and an inexperienced line showed steady improvement behind end Clay Matthews. "The numbers speak for

Sanchez is only the third quarterback to pass for more than 400 yards in a Rose Bowl, which he did in 2009. Ronald Johnson celebrates one of his TD catches on the cover of the Los Angeles Times *sports secction.*

themselves," California coach Jeff Tedford said. "They are as good as any I've seen."

With defense leading the way, the Trojans made one more run at the national title, winning by shutouts and one-sided scores through late November. But they were still paying for that early-season loss, stuck at No. 5 in the polls. Heading into the regular-season finale at UCLA, Carroll sought to downplay the BCS standings. "The goal of our program year in and year out has been to get to the Rose Bowl," he said. "We know that the Rose Bowl is within our control, and that's what we shoot for around here."

Mark Sanchez dives for a Rose Bowl score.

The crosstown rivalry turned out to be a surprisingly hard-fought game. Just like with Ohio State, USC surrendered an early score before clamping down. Sanchez threw a pair of touchdown passes,

The Trojans reached the 2009 Rose Bowl, making an unprecedented 33rd visit to Pasadena.

while tailbacks Joe McKnight and Stafon Johnson scored on the ground. The 28–7 victory—combined with an earlier Oregon State loss—gave the Trojans a record seventh consecutive Pacific-10 Conference title and a return trip to Pasadena to face Penn State on New Year's Day. As Carroll put it, "The BCS does what it does. We play the game."

"Hard to Beat"

The 2009 Rose Bowl wasn't nearly as close as the final score might suggest. Not with quarterback Mark Sanchez overcoming an early case of jitters to pass for 413 yards and four touchdowns. Not with the defense living up to its fearsome reputation. The Trojans opened a wide lead over Penn State, then coasted the rest of the way to a 38–24 victory on New Year's Day.

The Nittany Lions' venerable coach, Joe Paterno, called USC "as good a football team as there is in the country," which renewed the usual questions about national rankings and who deserved to hoist the championship trophy. Pete Carroll offered a simple response, a few words that explained not only the victory at hand but also the Trojans' rich heritage, their place among college football's elite. The same words could have been spoken by Howard Jones and John McKay before him. Carroll said: "We're just really, really hard to beat."

Troy Polamalu (his home jersey is pictured here) came to USC as an unheralded recruit and left as a two-time All-American.

This *Los Angeles Times* sports page shows moments of sheer joy as USC beats Oklahoma decisively, 55–19, to capture the 2005 national title.

In 2002, Troy Polamalu was awarded the cover of this homecoming issue for his outstanding performance his senior year.

This locker room sign, a trinket for fans, is ironic if only because the USC locker room is open to many different visitors.

This commemorative football was signed by members of the 2004 championship team.

A pennant from the 2009 Rose Bowl, where USC raced to a 38–24 victory over the Nittany Lions of Penn State.

The school's Trojan mascot takes a variety of shapes and forms, including this golf club headcover.

Record Book

RECORDS 1888–2008

Year	Overall Record	Conf. Record	Conf. Standing	Bowl	Year	Overall Record	Conf. Record	Conf. Standing	Bowl
1888	2–0–0	—			1915	3–4–0	—		
1889	2–0–0	—			1916	5–3–0	—		
1890	No Games				1917	4–2–1	—		
1891	1–2–0	—			1918	2–2–0	—		
1892	No Games				1919	4–1–0	—		
1893	3–1–0	—			1920	6–0–0	—		
1894	1–0–0	—			1921	10–1–0	—		
1895	0–1–1	—			1922	10–1–0	3–1–0	4	Rose
1896	0–3–0	—			1923	6–2–0	2–2–0	T3	—
1897	5–1-0	—			1924	9–2–0	2–1–0	T4	Christmas Festival
1898	5–1–1	—			1925	11–2–0	3–2–0	T3	—
1899	2–3–1	—			1926	8–2–0	5–1–0	2	—
1900	1–1–1	—			1927	8–1–1	4–0–1	T1	—
1901	0–1–0	—			1928	9–0–1	4–0–1	1	—
1902	2–3–0	—			1929	10–2–0	6–1–0	1	Rose
1903	4–2–0	—			1930	8–2–0	5–1–0	2	—
1904	6–1–0	—			1931	10–1–0	7–0–0	1	Rose
1905	6–3–1	—			1932	10–0–0	6–0–0	1	Rose
1906	2–0–2	—			1933	10–1–1	4–1–1	3	—
1907	5–1–0	—			1934	4–6–1	1–4–1	7	—
1908	3–1–1	—			1935	5–7–0	2–4–0	8	—
1909	3–1–2	—			1936	4–2–3	3–2–2	T3	—
1910	7–0–1	—			1937	4–4–2	2–3–2	7	—
1911	No Games (Rugby)				1938	9–2–0	6–1–0	T1	Rose
1912	No Games (Rugby)				1939	8–0–2	5–0–2	1	Rose
1913	No Games (Rugby)				1940	3–4–2	2–3–2	7	—
1914	4–3–0	—			1941	2–6–1	2–4–1	8	—

Year	Overall Record	Conf. Record	Conf. Standing	Bowl	Year	Overall Record	Conf. Record	Conf. Standing	Bowl
1942	5–5–1	4–2–1	4	—	1983	4–6–1	4–3–0	4	—
1943	8–2–0	5–0–0	1	Rose	1984	9–3–0	7–1–0	1	Rose
1944	8–0–2	3–0–2	1	Rose	1985	6–6–0	5–3–0	T4	Aloha
1945	7–4–0	5–1–0	1	Rose	1986	7–5–0	5–3–0	T4	Citrus
1946	6–4–0	5–2–0	3	—	1987	8–4–0	7–1–0	T1	Rose
1947	7–2–1	6–0–0	1	Rose	1988	10–2–0	8–0–0	1	Rose
1948	6–3–1	4–2–0	3	—	1989	9–2–1	6–0–1	1	Rose
1949	5–3–1	4–2–0	T3	—	1990	8–4–1	5–2–1	2	John Hancock
1950	2–5–2	1–3–2	7	—	1991	3–8–0	2–6–0	8	—
1951	7–3–0	4–2–0	4	—	1992	6–5–1	5–3–0	T3	Freedom
1952	10–1–0	6–0–0	1	Rose	1993	8–5–0	6–2–0	T1	Freedom
1953	6–3–1	4–2–1	3	—	1994	8–3–1	6–2–0	T2	Cotton
1954	8–4–0	6–1–0	2	Rose	1995	9–2–1	6–1–1	T1	Rose
1955	6–4–0	3–3–0	6	—	1996	6–6	3–5	T5	—
1956	8–2–0	5–2–0	T2	—	1997	6–5	4–4	T5	—
1957	1–9–0	1–6–0	T7	—	1998	8–5	5–3	T3	Sun
1958	4–5–1	4–2–1	3	—	1999	6–6	3–5	T6	—
1959	8–2–0	3–1–0	T1	—	2000	5–7	2–6	T8	—
1960	4–6–0	3–1–0	2	—	2001	6–6	5–3	5	Las Vegas
1961	4–5–1	2–1–1	T2	—	2002	11–2	7–1	T1	Orange
1962	11–0–0	4–0–0	1	Rose	2003	12–1	7–1	1	Rose
1963	7–3–0	3–1–0	2	—	2004	13–0	8–0	1	Orange
1964	7–3–0	3–1–0	T1	—	2005	12–1	8–0	1	Rose
1965	7–2–1	4–1–0	2	—	2006	11–2	7–2	T1	Rose
1966	7–4–0	4–1–0	1	Rose	2007	11–2	7–2	T1	Rose
1967	10–1–0	6–1–0	1	Rose	2008	12–1	8–1	1	Rose
1968	9–1–1	6–0–0	1	Rose					
1969	10–0–1	6–0–0	1	Rose					
1970	6–4–1	3–4–0	T6	—					
1971	6–4–1	3–2–1	2	—					
1972	12–0–0	7–0–0	1	Rose					
1973	9–2–1	7–0–0	1	Rose					
1974	10–1–1	6–0–1	1	Rose					
1975	8–4–0	3–4–0	5	Liberty					
1976	11–1–0	7–0–0	1	Rose					
1977	8–4–0	5–2–0	T2	Bluebonnet					
1978	12–1–0	6–1–0	1	Rose					
1979	11–0–1	6–0–1	1	Rose					
1980	8–2–1	4–2–1	3	—					
1981	9–3–0	5–2–0	T2	Fiesta					
1982	8–3–0	5–2–0	T3	—					

With the Rose Bowl on the line in 1939, USC and UCLA fought to a 0–0 tie in their annual showdown. The Trojans were chosen to go to the Rose Bowl, and they were declared national champions.

HEAD COACHES

Coach	Years	Record	Win Pct.
Henry Goddard & Frank Suffel	1888	2–0–0	1.000
Lewis Freeman	1897	5–1–0	.833
Clair Tappaan	1901	0–1–1	.000
John Walker	1903	4–2–0	.667
Harvey Holmes	1904–07	19–5–3	.759
William Traeger	1908	3–1–1	.700
Dean Cromwell	1909–10		
	1916–18	21–8–6	.686
Ralph Glaze	1914–15	7–7–0	.500
Elmer Henderson	1919–24	45–7–0	.865
Howard Jones	1925–40	121–36–13	.750
Sam Barry	1941	2–6–1	.278
Jeff Cravath	1942–50	54–28–8	.644
Jess Hill	1951–56	45–17–1	.722
Don Clark	1957–59	13–16–1	.450
John McKay	1960–75	127–40–8	.749
John Robinson	1976–82		
	1993–97	104–35–4	.741
Ted Tollner	1983–86	26–20–1	.564
Larry Smith	1987–92	44–25–3	.632
Paul Hackett	1998–2000	19–18–0	.514
Pete Carroll	2001–08	88–15	.854

This game ball is from the 1982 Fiesta Bowl. USC played Penn State.

BOWL GAME RESULTS

Year	Bowl	Result
1923	Rose	USC 14, Penn State 3
1924	Christmas Festival	USC 20, Missouri 7
1930	Rose	USC 47, Pittsburgh 14
1932	Rose	USC 21, Tulane 12
1933	Rose	USC 35, Pittsburgh 0
1939	Rose	USC 7, Duke 3
1940	Rose	USC 14, Tennessee 0
1944	Rose	USC 29, Washington 0
1945	Rose	USC 25, Tennessee 0
1946	Rose	Alabama 34, USC 14
1948	Rose	Michigan 49, USC 0
1953	Rose	USC 7, Wisconsin 0
1955	Rose	Ohio State 20, USC 7
1963	Rose	USC 42, Wisconsin 37
1967	Rose	Purdue 14, USC 13
1968	Rose	USC 14, Indiana 3
1969	Rose	Ohio State 27, USC 16
1970	Rose	USC 10, Michigan 3
1973	Rose	USC 42, Ohio State 17
1974	Rose	Ohio State 42, USC 21
1975	Rose	USC 18, Ohio State 17
1975	Liberty	USC 20, Texas A&M 0
1977	Rose	USC 14, Michigan 6
1977	Bluebonnet	USC 47, Texas A&M 28
1979	Rose	USC 17, Michigan 10
1980	Rose	USC 17, Ohio State 16
1982	Fiesta	Penn State 26, USC 10
1985	Rose	USC 20, Ohio State 17
1985	Aloha	Alabama 24, USC 3
1987	Citrus	Auburn 16, USC 7
1988	Rose	Michigan State 20, USC 17
1989	Rose	Michigan 22, USC 14
1990	Rose	USC 17, Michigan 10
1990	Hancock	Michigan State 17, USC 16
1992	Freedom	Fresno State 24, USC 7
1993	Freedom	USC 28, Utah 21
1995	Cotton	USC 55, Texas Tech 14
1996	Rose	USC 41, Northwestern 32
1998	Sun	TCU 28, USC 19
2001	Las Vegas	Utah 10, USC 6
2003	Orange	USC 38, Iowa 17
2004	Rose	USC 28, Michigan 14
2005	Orange (BCS)	USC 55, Oklahoma 19
2006	Rose (BCS)	Texas 41, USC 38
2007	Rose	USC 32, Michigan 18
2008	Rose	USC 49, Illinois 17
2009	Rose	USC 38, Penn State 24

USC PLAYERS IN THE COLLEGE FOOTBALL HALL OF FAME

Marcus Allen, 1978–81
Jon Arnett, 1954–56
John Baker, 1929–31
Ricky Bell, 1973–76
Tay Brown, 1930–32
Brad Budde, 1976–79
Paul Cleary, 1946–47
Anthony Davis, 1972–74
Morley Drury, 1925–27
John Ferraro, 1943–47
Mike Garrett, 1963–65
Frank Gifford, 1949–51
Mort Kaer, 1924–26
Ronnie Lott, 1977–80

Mike McKeever, 1958–60
Dan McMillan, 1917–19*
Erny Pinckert, 1929–31
Marvin Powell, 1974–76
Aaron Rosenberg, 1931–33
O. J. Simpson, 1967–68
Ernie Smith, 1930–32
Harry Smith, 1937–39
Lynn Swann, 1971–73
Cotton Warburton, 1932–34
Charles White, 1976–79
Richard Wood, 1972–74
Ron Yary, 1965–67
Charles Young, 1970–72

Finished career at California

HEISMAN TROPHY WINNERS

Mike Garrett, 1965
O. J. Simpson, 1968
Charles White, 1979
Marcus Allen, 1981

Carson Palmer, 2002
Matt Leinart, 2004
Reggie Bush, 2005

USC CONSENSUS ALL-AMERICANS

1926	Mort Kaer, B	1944	John Ferraro, T
1927	Morley Drury, B	1947	Paul Cleary, E
	Jess Hibbs, T	1952	Jim Sears, DB
1930	Erny Pinckert, B		Elmer Willhoite, G
1931	Johnny Baker, G	1962	Hal Bedsole, E
	Gus Shaver, B	1965	Mike Garrett, TB
1932	Ernie Smith, T	1966	Nate Shaw, DB
1933	Aaron Rosenberg, G		Ron Yary, OT
	Cotton Warburton, B	1967	O. J. Simpson, TB
1939	Harry Smith, G		Ron Yary, OT
1943	Ralph Heywood, E		Adrian Young, LB

	Tim Rossovich, DE	1984	Jack Del Rio, LB
1968	O. J. Simpson, TB	1985	Jeff Bregel, OG
1969	Jimmy Gunn, DE	1986	Jeff Bregel, OG
1970	Charles Weaver, DE		Tim McDonald, DB
1972	Charles Young, TE	1987	Dave Cadigan, OT
1973	Lynn Swann, FL	1989	Mark Carrier, DB
	Richard Wood, LB		Tim Ryan, DT
	Booker Brown, OT	1993	Johnnie Morton, WR
	Artimus Parker, DB	1994	Tony Boselli, OT
1974	Anthony Davis, TB	1995	Keyshawn Johnson, WR
	Richard Wood, LB	1998	Chris Claiborne, LB
1975	Ricky Bell, TB	2002	Carson Palmer, QB
1976	Ricky Bell, TB		Troy Polamalu, DB
	Dennis Thurman, DB	2003	Mike Williams, WR
	Gary Jeter, DT		Jacob Rogers, OT
1977	Dennis Thurman, DB		Kenechi Udeze, DE
1978	Pat Howell, OG	2004	Reggie Bush, TB
	Charles White, TB		Matt Leinart, QB
1979	Charles White, TB		Shaun Cody, DT
	Brad Budde, OG		Matt Grootegoed, LB
1980	Ronnie Lott, DB	2005	Reggie Bush, TB
	Keith Van Horne, OT		Dwayne Jarrett, WR
1981	Marcus Allen, TB		Taitusi Lutui, OG
	Roy Foster, OG	2006	Dwayne Jarrett, WR
1982	Don Mosebar, OT		Sam Baker, OT
	Bruce Matthews, OG	2007	Sedrick Ellis, DT
	George Achica, NG	2008	Rey Maualuga, LB
1983	Tony Slaton, C		Taylor Mays, DB

SCHOOL RECORDS & STATISTICAL LEADERS

Career Rushing

	Carries	Yards	Avg.
Charles White	1,147	6,245	5.44
Marcus Allen	932	4,810	5.16
Anthony Davis	784	3,724	4.75
Ricky Bell	710	3,689	5.20
O. J. Simpson	674	3,423	5.08
Mike Garrett	612	3,221	5.27
Reggie Bush	433	3,169	7.32

LenDale White	541	3,159	5.84
Fred Crutcher	670	2,815	4.20
Sultan McCullough	611	2,800	4.58

Career Passing

	Attempts	Comp.	Yards	Pct.
Carson Palmer	1,569	927	11,818	59.1
Matt Leinart	1,245	807	10,693	64.8
Rob Johnson	1,046	676	8,472	64.6
Rodney Peete	1,081	630	8,225	58.3
John David Booty	832	518	6,125	62.3
Todd Marinovich	674	415	5,001	61.6
Brad Otton	718	410	5,359	57.1
Sean Salisbury	602	346	4,481	57.5
Mark Sanchez	487	313	3,965	64.3
Paul McDonald	501	299	4,138	59.7

Career Receiving

	No.	Yards	Average
Dwayne Jarrett	216	3,138	14.53
Keary Colbert	207	2,964	14.32
Kareem Kelly	204	3,104	15.22
Johnnie Morton	201	3,201	15.93
Steve Smith	190	3,019	15.89
Mike Williams	176	2,579	14.65
Keyshawn Johnson	168	2,796	16.64
John Jackson	163	2,379	14.60
R. Jay Soward	161	2,672	16.60
Patrick Turner	138	1,752	12.70

Career Pass Interceptions

	No.	Yards	TDs
Artimus Parker	20	268	0
Danny Reece	18	228	1
Dennis Smith	16	225	0
Ronnie Lott	14	291	2
Bobby Robertson	14	157	0
Charles Phillips	13	365	3
Dennis Thurman	13	305	2
Bruce Dyer	13	149	1
Mike Battle	13	148	0
Mark Carrier	13	135	0

Career Total Offense

	Rush	Pass	Total
Carson Palmer	-197	11,818	11,621
Matt Leinart	-70	10,693	10,623
Rodney Peete	415	8,225	8,640
Rob Johnson	-576	8,472	7,896
Charles White	6,245	-5	6,240
John David Booty	-180	6,125	5,945
Brad Otton	-236	5,359	5,123
Marcus Allen	4,810	57	4,867
Todd Marinovich	-153	5,001	4,848
Jimmy Jones	409	4,092	4,501

SINGLE GAME RECORDS

Most points: 36, Anthony Davis, 1972 vs. Notre Dame

Most touchdowns: 6, Anthony Davis, 1972 vs. Notre Dame

Most field goals: 5, Ryan Killeen, 2004 vs. UCLA

Most rushing yards: 347, Ricky Bell, 1976 vs. Washington State

Most passing yards: 448, Carson Palmer, 2002 vs. Oregon

Most receiving yards: 260, R. Jay Soward, 1996 vs. UCLA

Most touchdowns on punt returns: 2, Mike Garrett, 1965 vs. California

Most passes intercepted: 4, Adrian Young, 1967 vs. Notre Dame

Most interception returns for touchdowns: 2, Jim Psaltis, 1952 vs. Washington State; Charles Phillips, 1974 vs. Iowa; Antuan Simmons, 1998 vs. Washington

Most sacks: 4, Marcus Cotton, 1987 vs. Oregon State; Junior Seau, 1989 vs. Oregon State; Tim Ryan, 1989 vs. UCLA; Lawrence Jackson, 2007 vs. Arizona State

LONG PLAY RECORDS

Longest run from scrimmage: 96 yards, LaVale Woods, 1996 vs. Oregon State

Longest pass play: 97 yards, Matt Koffler to R. Jay Soward, 1996 vs. Illinois

Longest field goal: 60 yards, Don Shafer, 1986 vs. Notre Dame

Longest kickoff returns: 100 yards, Anthony Davis, 1974 vs. Arkansas and Notre Dame. (In 1902, Elwin Caley returned a kick 107 yards vs. Pomona on a 110-yard field.)

Longest punt return: 96 yards, Curtis Conway, 1992 vs. Oregon

Longest punt: 85 yards, Ernie Zampese, 1956 vs. Wisconsin

Index